LONGING *for a* CHILD

Also by Kathe Wunnenberg

Grieving the Child I Never Knew
Grieving the Loss of a Loved One

DEVOTIONS OF HOPE
FOR YOUR *Journey* THROUGH INFERTILITY

Kathe Wunnenberg

LONGING *for a* CHILD

ZONDERVAN™

GRAND RAPIDS, MICHIGAN 49530 USA

Longing for a Child
Copyright © 2005 by Kathe Wunnenberg

Requests for information should be addressed to:
Zondervan, *Grand Rapids, Michigan 49530*

ISBN-10: 0-310-25665-8
ISBN-13: 978-0-310-25665-6 (hardcover)

This edition printed on acid-free paper.

All Scripture quotations, unless otherwise indicated, are taken from the *Holy Bible: New International Version®*. NIV®. Copyright © 1973, 1978, 1984 by International Bible Society. Used by permission of Zondervan. All rights reserved.

The website addresses recommended throughout this book are offered as a resource to you. These websites are not intended in any way to be or imply an endorsement on the part of Zondervan, nor do we vouch for their content for the life of this book.

Interior design by Michelle Espinoza

Printed in the United States of America

05 06 07 08 09 10 11 12 /❖ DCI/ 10 9 8 7 6 5 4 3 2 1

This book is lovingly dedicated to my mom, Alice Stephens,
and my Grannie, Jennie Young,
who longed for children and persevered.
Thank you for your faith, encouragement, and prayers.
Without you, this book would not be possible!
To God be the glory!

CONTENTS

Section 1
LONGING

Section 2
WONDERING

Section 3
WAITING

Section 8
TRUSTING

Section 9
RELEASING

Section 10
REDIRECTING

Section 11
ACCEPTING

Section 12
EMBRACING

Section 13
SPECIAL MEDITATIONS FOR SPECIAL DAYS

ACKNOWLEDGMENTS

Behind the pages of this book, a multitude of people supported me in my journey. Many choose to remain anonymous as my silent supporters. To those of you who know who you are . . . thank you!

Thanks to many of you who prayed for me at various stages throughout my writing; the list is too long to recount. A special thanks to my mom, Alice Stephens, my aunt Donna Gipson, Aunt Wilma, Carol Kent, Laura Withrow, Toni Paulich, and Darlene Adams.

To my Zondervan family—thank you for seeing the need for this book. To my editors, Cindy Hays Lambert, Evelyn Bence, and Verlyn Verbrugge, God's timing is *always* perfect, and your wisdom and ideas were too!

Thanks to The Vision Group, Jennie Saake, and Hannah's Prayer for your encouragement. A special thanks to Robert and Stephanie Melotti, Tim and Mary Ann Mejdrich, Jeff and Cindy Mugford, Trinka Henderson, Brenda Dull, Jan James, Debbie Mis, Sandra Saoud, Lisa Jernigan, Sara Perty, and my brother Doug Stephens for allowing me to share your personal stories.

To the staff at Starbucks at Ray and 51st Street in Chandler, Arizona—thanks for reserving my writing table and for lotsa lattes.

To my friends and family—thanks for your grace in understanding when I forgot occasions or failed to return your emails or calls in a timely fashion.

Jake, Josh, and Jordan—thanks for sharing Mommy and filling my arms and heart. John Samuel, Zachery, Matthew, and Luke, although I never knew you fully, some day I will. Your brief lives changed me and enlarged my compassion and faith. My husband, Rich—thanks for supporting me with your time and resources so I could write.

To my Lord and Savior Jesus Christ—without you I could not have endured my journey of longing for a child and completed the task to which you have called me.

How to Use This Book

L *onging for a Child* is designed with flexibility to meet needs unique to your personality. You may choose to read it daily or as the need arises; while undergoing fertility testing or years later; alone, with another person, or with a group. How you use this book is entirely up to you.

Similar to my first two books, *Grieving the Loss of a Loved One* and *Grieving the Child I Never Knew*, this book is divided into twelve sections with five devotions in each. Each devotion contains a Scripture passage, a short thematic story, a prayer, three to five gentle reflective questions, and a place to journal. At the end of the book, a special meditation section encourages you to read and reflect on appropriate Scriptures, quotes, or devotions and record your thoughts on days or occasions when you may need additional encouragement. A subsequent section helps you write your own personal story, and a final resource section contains additional organizations and tools to encourage you.

I have identified seven settings in which you might use this book.

Alone in the garden. Use *Longing for a Child* as your personal daily devotional. You may choose to read it start to finish systematically or turn to the Table of Contents and choose the section that matches your daily mood.

Two-getherness. Invite your spouse or a close friend to read and discuss the book with you. Choose a comfortable setting to meet regularly: your bedroom, your backyard, a park, or favorite restaurant or coffee house.

Dig with others. Join with others for a twelve-week Bible study. Dig into God's Word and truth by focusing on one section per week.

Weed with others. Invite your counselor or pastor to join you and read *Longing for a Child* together. As a counseling tool, my book can help you pluck out weeds that may be threatening your personal or spiritual growth and provide truth and perspective.

Bloom with others. Use the book as a discussion guide for a fertility support group that meets in person, by phone, or online. Invite others who also long for a child to connect and encourage one another.

For seasonal fertilizer. Various changes, occasions, or events may trigger your need to read or reread specific sections. As Mother's Day approaches or you venture into a new season of your longing, you may sense a need for encouragement. Refer to the special meditation section or special readings/special days section.

For a group—workshop, women's event, or weekend. Help others who also long for a child or desire to encourage those who do by hosting an interactive *Longing for a Child* gathering: a workshop, women's event, or weekend retreat. Invite me to join you personally and inspire you and your group with messages from this book. Contact speakupspeakerservices.com or zondervan.com for more information about creating a customized experience to meet your group's unique needs.

Introduction

My mother is an avid gardener. Her yard, a mini Garden of Eden, is in the foothills to the Ozarks and overlooks Castor River in Marquand, Missouri. It is lush with towering trees, cascading plants, and flowers that are colorful in season. Her pantry is filled with jars of homegrown vegetables. I've always marveled at her ability to nurture and grow plants from clippings, seeds, or bulbs. Unfortunately I didn't receive her green thumb gift and lack the patience and perseverance required for gardening. I'm embarrassed to admit that "silk" flowers have a place in my backyard in Arizona. Yet despite our differences and the distance that separates us, Mom and I have always been close in spirit. We have supported each other through encouragement and prayer, though we have lived apart for more than twenty years.

Throughout my journey of longing for a child and losing four children, Mom nurtured me with her presence and watered my grieving soul with her faith and tears. I always knew she was there for me, though I'm not sure I voiced my appreciation as much as I could have.

Recently I got homesick for Mom and took a break from writing to visit her. Little did I know God would use this trip to inspire the introduction for this book. For several days I enjoyed Mom's home cooking, flavored coffee, and outings with her to the senior center, Ms. Allison's store, church, and The Hideaway Café. Together we pored over the pages of the first draft for this book.

While we worked, we reflected on our family's history and the women before us—my grannie and great-grandmother—who had longed for and lost children. Even my mother, though she never considered herself to be fertility challenged, unknowingly suffered "secondary infertility" after the birth of my older brother, Danny. Because her labor and delivery had been so difficult, she was satisfied to have only one child. But when she attended the funeral of an only son and saw the parents' unspeakable grief, something within her nudged her to reconsider.

Not quickly, but finally Mom conceived. When she miscarried early in her pregnancy, she endured her loss in silence; people of her generation did not share openly about pregnancies or fertility challenges. Mom did not give up but became even more determined to have a second child. She journeyed frequently to see a doctor many miles away. Monthly disappointments did not stop her. Her perseverance finally paid off.

When Danny was almost six years old, she finally delivered a healthy baby daughter: Kathe Lynne Homan. The seed of faith and hope God planted in her heart finally blossomed into a child. I am grateful that Mom listened to the still, small voice of God and opened up her heart to allow herself to long for another child. Without Mom and the women in my family before her, who also longed for children and persevered, you would not be reading this book.

I will never have a daughter of my own, but God has planted sons in the garden of my life to nurture. My oldest son was grafted into our family through adoption in 1989 and our two younger sons were born to me in my forties, after nearly twenty years of marriage, years of fertility challenges, and the loss of an infant son and of three other children through miscarriage.

My story is different from yours, but the pages of our lives share a common theme. Silent suffering. The longing for a child. You may well experience different seasons of yearning for a child to hold, to love, and to continue your family's legacy. At different stages of your life, you may feel different emotions about your child or your longing.

Perhaps you are in the spring of your journey; you have just decided to have a child. You can picture the lush, green landscape of what your family should look like. Although you water your desire with faith, hope, and prayer, your backyard remains barren. Will a child ever grow there? As time passes, you may become discouraged as you wait for the seed of your longing to sprout. This book will encourage you as you seek truth and information about infertility.

Is the heat of summer scorching your hope? Do you feel as if the insects of introspection and indifference are threatening to destroy you? Was your child conceived and growing, only to be uprooted from your womb? Or do you feel as if your circumstances are hopeful, but you're afraid to smell the fragrance of hope because of past disappointments? I pray my book will water you with Living Water of truth and encouragement.

Is time running out? Do you feel as if you are facing the autumn, a critical time before winter when you may have to make difficult choices about your fertility? Is God directing you to let go of your plans and encouraging you to plant the bulb of a different kind in the garden of your desires? Are you weary from waiting? Will you ever experience harvest time and have a child? Perhaps time has changed your perspective. As your leaves of hope fall to the ground, is God causing you to reflect and consider different options? My book will cheer you on to help you persevere and consider new directions.

Or do you feel as if all hope has died? Are you grieving the death of your child or your longing for a child? Because of circumstances beyond your control, are you forced to face a reality different from the one you had planned? Are you at the end of your emotions, finances, relationship, or physical options? Has your faith died?

Perhaps you are experiencing a season of winter and do not believe spring will ever come. The ground of your garden is frozen with hopelessness, regret, or fear. Winter is a season of surrender and rest. It may also be a time to regroup and allow God to restore you and prepare you for a spring of a different kind than you imagined. Perhaps hope is budding just beneath the surface even though you don't see it yet. I pray my book will warm you with compassion and renew your faith in God's miracle-working power and come alongside of you in the garden of your life, no matter what season you are in.

Although I don't understand everything you are going through, I can relate to some of what you are experiencing as you long for a child. Think of my book as your companion of hope, a ray of sunshine, to shine truth, encouragement, and perspective on your situation. Many fellow strugglers who have also longed for a child have willingly shared their stories to help you grow through your longing. My prayer is that my book will give you a feeling of "going home" to a comfortable, secure place where you feel loved and accepted.

As you read each devotion, imagine your heavenly Father wrapping his loving arms around you. Experience his presence and truth. He understands your longing, and he will meet you where you are and help you grow. He will be with you through every season of your journey and will help you bloom wherever you are planted. May God meet you in the garden of your life and reveal to you hidden beauty from your experience.

In time perhaps you will allow him to use you to plant hope in another person's garden. My prayer is that God will do immeasurably more than all you ask or imagine in your life and through your longing for a child, according to his power within you. Let's begin the journey.

LONGING

*Longing: A strong, persistent desire or craving
for something unattainable or distant.*

*Delight yourself in the Lord
  and he will give you the desires of your heart.*
                                        Psalm 37:4

*My soul is in anguish.
  How long, O LORD, how long? . . .
I am worn out from groaning,
  all night long I flood my bed with weeping
  and drench my couch with tears. . . .
The LORD has heard my cry for mercy;
  the LORD accepts my prayer.*
                                    Psalm 6:3, 6, 9

*All my longings lie open before you, O Lord;
  my sighing is not hidden from you.*
                                        Psalm 38:9

JOURNEY TO THE DUNES OF DESIRE

The LORD himself goes before you and will be with you; he will never leave you nor forsake you. Do not be afraid; do not be discouraged.

Deuteronomy 31:8

When our veteran "duner" friends Mark and Stephanie invited us to join their family for a weekend at the Imperial Sand Dunes, we accepted. It was the perfect opportunity to try out our new twenty-six-foot trailer with bath and shower amenities (a must for me!)—sporting our two new quads. Clad in my new steel-toed boots, matching chest protector, gloves, and helmet, I mounted my quad and pushed the start button. VRMMMMM...

The Imperial Dunes extend for more than forty miles in southern California, southwestern Arizona, and into Mexico. Mountain-sized mounds of sand range from two to six miles in width, with crests rising two to three hundred feet above the surrounding landscape. Hollywood cameras have depicted these dunes as the desert for numerous war scenes and science-fiction planets. A popular winter destination for sports enthusiasts, the Dunes buzz with sand rails, buggies, quads, and motorcycles. The seemingly endless sandscape is beautiful, thrilling, eerie, treacherous.

Although I had ridden motorcycles in the Midwest during my youth, my forty-something body was unfamiliar with the quad's finger throttles and paddle tires . . . and the sand. Could I maneuver this terrain or would I crash? My stomach churned with excitement and anxiety. My mind swirled with uncertainty as I released the clutch and sputtered behind my friend Stephanie. I felt comfortable driving along the flat, open road of sand. *I can do this!* I thought. Then I saw the iceberg of sand rising up in front of me. Stephanie maneuvered her quad effortlessly up and over.

Fear gripped me. *Should I turn back?* I waited. Then I looked up and saw Stephanie at the top of the crest waving me on. I gulped. I opened the throttle, and moments later I was beside her. During the next few hours we traversed over the crests and through the canyons of sand. As I sped behind the pack across the open plain, I sensed something familiar about this journey. It seemed similar to my quest to have a child.

In the camp with other childless sojourners and robed with a new attire of perspectives, attitudes, feelings, and terminology, I had faced the Dunes of My Desire. At times the ride was exhilarating. At other times, exasperating. Nearing each crest, I wondered what lay waiting for me on the other side. I experienced a repeating cycle of fear and dread followed by accomplishment and hope. Fueled by my desire, I was able to keep going, no matter how endless and treacherous the terrain seemed. Though at times I wanted to turn back, I continued. Looking up I could always find someone at the top of the crest who had climbed the mountain I was facing, waving me on.

Where are you in your journey? Perhaps this is your first encounter, and you are camped at the foot of the Dunes, ready to gear up and go. Or perhaps you've been riding through the sands of uncertainty for a long time, lost with no end in sight. Maybe you are facing a three hundred-foot mountain today and don't know if you have what it takes to make it up the slope. Maybe you are plummeting down into a canyon.

Wherever you are, just know that you are not alone, though at times you may feel as if you are. God is there—and others are too. Look up! Just when you think you can't make it, you may see someone standing at the top of the mountain cheering you on. That's where I am now. Picture me waving you on and shouting, "You can do it!" Ready. Set. VRMMMMMM...

Lord, I feel as if I'm facing an endless journey. I'm afraid. I've never done this before, and I don't like feeling uncomfortable and uncertain. Help me in my journey. Guide my ride. Give me courage. Thank you for providing others to cheer me on. Fuel me with your Word and wisdom as I face the Dunes of Desire to have a child. Amen.

Steps toward Growth

1. Reflect on where you are in your journey. At the campsite? Ready to ride? Riding up? At the base of one dune with another to face? At the top of a crest? Over the final crest?
2. Reread Deuteronomy 31:8. How does this verse encourage you?
3. Read Matthew 14:26–27 as if Jesus were speaking to you personally.
4. Picture Jesus at the top of a dune waving you on. What steps will you take this week to have courage and continue in your ride?

My Personal Journey

Father I feel sad and overwhelmed w/grief
My heart is heavy. I long for a child
Jesus + my child I need to lay this down
do a work in me during this difficult
time - restore my joy - help me to see
others that are hurting - I surrender the
desires of my heart - we want a healthy
baby Lord - Open our eyes as to how this
can happen - Make our path crystal clear
Adoption or pregnancy - We can only do this
thigh you - Surround me with your peace

All my longings lie open before you, O, LORD.
My sighing is not hidden from you.

Psalm 38:9

"All I ever wanted was to become a mom," sobbed Trinka.

Instinctively, I handed her a tissue and gave her a reassuring hug. My heart was breaking for my friend as I listened to her recall her doctor's visit earlier that day.

"Kathe, he said I would *never* be able to have a child. He made me feel like a freak!"

How familiar this conversation felt. Just months earlier, I too had received devastating news after I had miscarried our first child in 1989. Several tests and doctor visits later produced a "We don't know if you'll ever be able to have a child" report.

At that moment I wish I could have waved a magic wand and fulfilled Trinka's desire. I knew that nothing I could say would ease her pain. Instead of words, I offered her my silence and my tears. We wept together. Two wannabe moms.

Longing to be a mom can be a lonely journey at times. When you look around, you may feel as if you're the only one who doesn't have a child. The desire of your heart is to have and hold a child, to gaze into a tiny face, to tickle toes, and to be awakened in the middle of the night. Yet no child comes and the longing intensifies.

Will the desire for a child ever go away? I don't know. The wannabe-a-mom journey is personal and unique for every woman. Although I can relate to some of what you are feeling, I don't know exactly how you feel.

Will you ever have a child? I don't know.

Will you ever receive the answers to your questions? I don't know.

Should you persevere in your attempts to have a child or give up? I don't know.

Is there hope for you? Absolutely!

You're not alone in your trek. Wannabe moms are everywhere. Open your eyes.

She may be your coworker, the woman next to you in the grocery store line, your neighbor, or your friend. Like you, she has a longing in her heart and is waiting silently for it to be filled. Should she wait in silence or could you be the person God is calling to walk beside her?

I think often of the Old Testament story of Sarah, who was childless into her old age. I wonder whom she talked to every month when she discovered she wasn't pregnant *again*! As the years passed, did a faithful wannabe-a-mom friend share her silence and her tears? Did she remind Sarah of God's promise to her and encourage her to look to him as her strength and support?

Like you, I never planned to be among the wannabe moms, but for many years, there I was. I dreaded Mother's Day, baby showers, friends who announced "I'm pregnant," doctors' visits, family gatherings, hurtful comments, people who asked, "How many children do you have?" temperature charts, brown paper bags, another ovulation kit, that "knowing look," and another birthday without a child.

I'm willing to be your companion in your wannabe-a-mom journey. Through the pages of my book, I hope we share laughter and tears, comfort and hope. I will be your cheerleader, who points you to the One who hears your cries. No matter what you are facing, God is there and he is good. He understands your longing for a child and will guide your steps. He cares about you—and so do I.

God, will I ever be a mom? Only you know the answer to this question. All my longings lie open before you. My wannabe-a-mom heart aches with uncertainty. Be my comforting companion and my hope. Open my eyes to others who understand my silent suffering. Guide my steps. Amen.

Steps toward Growth

1. When and how have you felt alone in your journey to have a child?
2. What could others do to encourage you most right now?
3. In your circle of acquaintances do you know any other wannabe moms? How could you encourage those women?
4. What do you hope to receive from the experience of reading this devotional book?
5. Read Psalm 40 aloud. What words and/or phrases encourage you most about this Scripture?

My Personal Journey

_____

_____

_____

_____

_____

_____

_____

_____

_____

_____

_____

_____

_____

Devotion 3

STOLEN IDENTITY?

The Spirit himself testifies with our spirit that we are God's children. Now if we are children, then we are heirs—heirs of God and co-heirs with Christ, if indeed we share in his sufferings in order that we may also share in his glory.

Romans 8:16–17

Kathe, I have *your* driver's license!" announced my god-daughter Sara, who lived a few blocks from the park where I was watching my son's baseball game.

I clutched my cell phone closer to my ear so I could hear. *What?* My mind whirled with questions. "How did you get it?"

"My boyfriend found your driver's license lying near the street when he was walking home from work tonight," Sara replied.

Oh dear! I hurried to the parking lot, where I'd locked my purse in the car. Outwardly my car appeared undisturbed, but . . . my purse and everything in it, including my Daytimer, had been stolen. Rich and I spent the next several hours canceling accounts, filing police reports, calling credit bureaus, opening new bank accounts, and praying that our efforts would prevent my identity from being stolen too.

If you've ever been robbed, you can relate to the sick, helpless feeling that accompanies the wave of emotions, blame, and questions. Perhaps you've never lost possessions, but you feel as if a promotion, relationship, education, or dream has been stolen from you. As a victim of life's circumstances or choices, you may feel as if a part of who you hoped to become—in a sense, your identity—has been taken. Even though you may cry out, seek help, and try to make the most of your life, at times you feel incomplete, as if the thief has ransacked your life.

I think of the Old Testament story found in the book of Ruth. A dejected Naomi had lost her husband and sons—and a part of herself too. The thief of death had stolen her identity as a wife and mother and her future hope of becoming a grandmother. Her heart must have ached with a void. She would never cuddle wee ones on her lap, or tell them stories, or tuck them into bed at night. Robbed of a future legacy and robed in aloneness, she decided to move back to her home country.

To Naomi's surprise her daughter-in-law Ruth insisted that she would follow Naomi. "Where you go, I will go, and where you stay I will stay. Your people will be my people and your God my God" (Ruth 1:16). How comforted Naomi must have felt to hear Ruth speak these words. In her brokenness, God provided a companion of hope whom God chose to use to bless Naomi and restore her stolen identity.

Do you feel as if part of your identity has been stolen? When you try to identify your inner longings, do you feel as if your anticipated role as a parent or grandparent has been snatched? Like Naomi, you may be a victim of life's circumstances and are barely surviving in a barren, broken place. Maybe you've become so obsessed with trying to have a child that you've also lost track of professional identity.

Maybe it's time to step back and reassess the most basic elements of your identity. Who are you? Scripture has a lot to say about a Christian's identity. You are:

- A beloved child of God ("How great is the love the Father has lavished on us, that we should be called children of God!" 1 John 3:1).
- A needed member of the body of Christ ("Now you are the body of Christ, and each one of you is a part of it," 1 Corinthians 12:27).
- A carefully crafted creation of God in Christ ("We are God's workmanship, created in Christ Jesus to do good works, which God prepared in advance for us to do," Ephesians 2:10).

- The bride of Christ ("For the wedding of the Lamb has come, and his bride has made herself ready," Revelation 19:7).
- A letter from Christ ("You show that you are a letter from Christ," 2 Corinthians 3:3).

Ask God today to remind you of your identity in him. Then guard it well.

Lord, help! I've been robbed of my identity as a _____. My future hopes have been stolen. Even my present identity has become blurred. Remind me of who I am in Christ. Help me to guard that basic identity, no matter what threats or losses I feel or experience today. Amen.

STEPS TOWARD GROWTH

1. What role or "identity" do you feel has been stolen from you? From others in your family?

2. Read the Old Testament book of Ruth. Look for clues to Naomi's changing sense of identity, first based in bitter hopelessness, but eventually tied to the One who became her Restorer-Redeemer.

3. List as many positive self-identities as you can think of—based on Scripture and also based on positive realities of your life. Review the list and write or say a prayer that summarizes the identity that represents God's blessing in your life.

MY PERSONAL JOURNEY

Father God   Help me to find other
wamakemans - fill my hole + work with
you Father please forgive me - I
am so sad now - so confused
We have been told - that we have
pretty much no chance to get pregnat

Devotion 4
THE EMPTY PORTRAIT

*I have been reminded of your sincere faith, which first lived in
your grandmother Lois and in your mother Eunice and, I am
persuaded, now lives in you also.*

2 Timothy 1:5

Family portraits adorn the walls in my mother's home. One special group-
ing features my grandmother, my mother, and me—three generations of
hazel-eyed sixteen-year-olds, a tradition I planned to continue when my daughter became sixteen. My hopes dimmed with each passing year.

I married my college sweetheart, Rich, four days before my twenty-second
birthday in 1980. Children were not part of our early marriage plans. In fact, I
was reluctant to have children at all. (I discuss this in greater detail in Devotion
37, "Is God Punishing Me?") However, God changed my heart in my late twenties and I hoped to achieve motherhood by age thirty. Two years and three
rounds of Clomid later, I became pregnant, but I miscarried our first child when
I was twenty-nine.

Simultaneously we started the adoption process while undergoing fertility
testing. After a couple of years, when I was thirty-one, we adopted Jacob (Jake)
Paul Wunnenberg. At that time, I wanted a son and pictured myself as a "boy"
mom.

During the next ten years, I suffered the loss of a child shortly after birth
plus I had two more miscarriages. Eventually the Lord did bless me with two
full-term pregnancies—Joshua and then Jordan. We sensed God's peace that
our family was complete. I feel blessed to have sons, and I never felt the void of

a daughter until I began writing this book. Only then did I grieve the daughter I will never know.

Each time I gaze at the empty portrait space on my mother's wall, I realize the family tradition has ended with me. I will never have the joy of seeing my hazel-eyed daughter's portrait displayed next to mine.

Longing to pass on your heritage, family traits, or traditions to your children seems naturally ingrained in our psyches. We take the matter for granted until we consider what life would be like if we don't have children. Have you ever thought about future generations? What family trait or traditions do you imagine your children's children's children will continue? Perhaps it's red hair, dimples, or hazel eyes. Or your family name, business, heirlooms, occupation, hobbies, recipes, or a portrait. Give yourself permission to think about what you hope to pass along.

Will you ever have a child to carry on your name? I don't know. It's okay to feel deeply for the child you may never know and your future generations. Perhaps God will call you, like Rich and me, to adopt a child. Although this is a great joy for some, not all couples feel led to do this. Even if you do choose to adopt, you may still grieve the loss of your biological heritage.

Let yourself grieve, even as you hope for and continue to imagine the child that will fill out the family you desire. I see this pattern in the Old Testament story of Hannah, who desperately prayed for a child. Even as she did so, she dedicated that child—and his future—to God and his service; "I will give him to the LORD for all the days of his life," she prayed (1 Samuel 1:11). That was the heritage most important to her—that the child be in God's house, in God's family, in God's family portrait.

Perhaps, in time, like Hannah, God will fill your arms, but is he asking you to commit your future child to him today even before your child is conceived? How wise it is to place your most precious longings into God's hands to use for his glory.

Lord, I'm blinded by my pain. I want to pass on my traits and traditions to my children, but all I see is an empty portrait on the wall. Will our family future stop with me? Do you have a different plan? I want what you want, even though it's hard to imagine life without children of my own. Lord, please give me a child.

Today I commit my future children to you. May any child you choose to give me serve you, glorify you, and multiply your kingdom. Amen.

STEPS TOWARD GROWTH

1. What family traits or traditions do you hope to pass on to your children?
2. What do you think your child would look like? Act like? Become?
3. Grieving the loss of someone you may never know is normal. Consider writing a letter to this child and the hopes and dreams you have. Include spiritual aspects of this dream and your dedication of the child to God and his service.
4. Read Isaiah 25:8 and 61:1–3. What comfort can you see in these verses?

MY PERSONAL JOURNEY

I dream of a child who will be in sports, 4-H
Enjoy the blessing of life. A boy with
blond hair and blue eyes. Father God I
dedicate this child to you — to serve
and love you — He will grow up to
serve you in an awesome way. Lord please
give us a child. Make it clean in our hearts

MY PERSONAL JOURNEY

which path to take. Father, forgive
me for losing hope. I want to focus
on loving and serving you. Open my eyes
on how I can do that. Father my
heart is breaking - I feel as if there
is a Gov valley between you + I. Help
to heal that and make our path clear.
We love you Lord - we desire to
do your will. If it is your will for
us to not have a child - please fill
this hole in my heart

Devotion 5

THE FATHER LONGS FOR YOU

But while he was still a long way off, his father saw him and was filled with compassion for him; he ran to his son, threw his arms around him and kissed him.

Luke 15:20b

I *miss my son*, the man thought as he gazed at the empty chair. *I miss everything about him: his dark, wavy hair, his penetrating eyes, the way his nostrils flared when he was angry, his spontaneous laughter, his zany sense of humor, his impulsive, carefree personality, and his persistent, probing questions.* He chuckled as he recalled their lively conversations. *My youngest son is definitely my "why child." He demands an explanation for everything, unlike his older brother who follows my rules without complaint. When my youngest son asked for his future inheritance NOW, I didn't hesitate and gave it to him, even though I knew he would leave home.*

The father wiped a tear from his cheek as he opened the front door and walked outside. A gentle morning breeze greeted him with the aroma of fresh-tilled fields, budding trees, and spring flowers. An orchestra of birds chirped a springtime melody. The father stared at the dirt road that stretched through the endless acres of farmland. His heart swelled with hope each sunrise and faded at sunset.

Day after day he waited, longing for his son to return home. He yearned to wrap his arms around his son again and tell him how deeply he loved him. The void he felt deep within his soul could not be fully satisfied. Nothing could ever take his son's place. He closed his eyes and imagined his son's return ... "Father, Father, I'm home." Perhaps, *today* will be the day.

The story of the prodigal son found in Luke 15:11–32 is one of my childhood favorites. I identified with the story then because I lived in the country and had two pet pigs, Lynden and LadyBird. (Guess who was president then?) I knew what pigs ate, and I couldn't imagine any human wanting to dine that way. As I grew, so did my personal insights about this story. I always seemed to see the story from one of the son's perspectives—the younger, adventure-seeking son or the goody-goody son with the finger-pointing, critical spirit. I wavered back and forth between the two sons through my growing-up years.

It wasn't until after I was married and was trying to conceive a child that my eyes were opened to the father's perspective. I identified with his intense longing for his child. He longed for his younger son to return physically home, and I think he also longed for his older son to come home with a different attitude. More important, my heart began to understand the immense unconditional love a father has for his child. No matter what a child does or says, a father still loves him. A father waits patiently with open arms to welcome home his child.

Have you ever stopped to think about that? This has always been a difficult truth for me to grasp, partly because of my personal experience of my parent's divorce when I was a child and I was forced to live apart from my father. Though I knew my earthly father loved me, he didn't always express it to me in the manner I desired. Dad's quiet, nonintrusive nature at times made me feel unloved. However, I've come to realize much like the father in the story, my dad patiently endured my absence and always welcomed me home with open arms.

Romans 8:35, 38–39 says that nothing can separate us from the love of God that is in Christ Jesus our Lord. Nothing you have done, or said, will make God love you less. He is your Father, the one who made you. He loves everything about you! Even if you doubt his love because he hasn't filled your arms with a child, nothing will ever separate you from his love. No matter how deeply you long for a child, God longs for you to be his child and come to his home, even more. He is waiting with open arms to embrace you with his love right now.

Is today the day? Think about it. He loved you so much that he sent his only Son, Jesus, to become a man and to die a horrible death on a cross for your sins. But God's love didn't stop there. He raised Jesus from the dead and has him preparing a heavenly home for you, his child. Is it time to accept his love and assurance of a heavenly home?

Even if you know God as your Father, have you kept your distance and lived apart from him? Or maybe you've left home with an attitude and pointed a critical finger at him, and you need to receive his forgiving love. It's time to go home. Your Father longs for you. He loves you more than words can express. He has been patiently waiting for you to come to him. Now's the time. Go home. Allow your Father to embrace you with his everlasting love today.

Father, I need you in my life. I need your unconditional love. Forgive me for my wrong thoughts, actions, and attitudes. Thank you for expressing your love for me through Jesus and providing me an eternal home with you. Embrace me with your everlasting arms. Help me receive your love fully today and live at home with you in my life. You are my Father, and I am the child you long for. Amen.

STEPS TOWARD GROWTH

1. Read the story of the prodigal son in Luke 15:11–32. Which character do you identify with? Why?

2. The Father longs for you as his child. How does this encourage you?

3. God is love. Read 1 John 4:7–18. Insert your name and read them as if God wrote these verses to you personally. Circle any words that are meaningful.

4. Look for ways God is expressing love to you personally this week. Perhaps you'll receive a word, song, gift, unexpected call, or visit from someone. Perhaps you will see a beautiful sunset, or perhaps God will express love in an intangible way by providing extra patience, peace, or courage.

5. Express love to your Father this week by being present with him. Talk and listen to him for ten to fifteen minutes each day. When and where will you embrace him?

MY PERSONAL JOURNEY

_____

_____

_____

_____

_____

_____

_____

_____

_____

_____

_____

_____

_____

_____

_____

_____

_____

_____

_____

_____

_____

_____

_____

_____

_____

_____

_____

WONDERING

Wondering: *To think or speculate curiously and sometimes doubtfully.*

Why, O LORD, do you stand far off?
  Why do you hide yourself in times of trouble?

Psalm 10:1

[Jesus] said to them, "Why are you troubled, and why do doubts rise in your minds?"

Luke 24:38

Jesus asked them, "What do you think about the Christ?"

Matthew 22:42a

Devotion 6

WHO'S TO BLAME?

Then Job replied to the LORD:
"I know that you can do all things;
    no plan of yours can be thwarted.
You asked, 'Who is this that obscures my counsel without
knowledge?'
        Surely I spoke of things I did not understand,
        things too wonderful for me to know."

Job 42:2–3

"L ights! Camera! Action!" An ocean of applause responds as the game show host walks on stage. "Welcome to *The Blame Game*," he says.

The curtains rise and four contestant couples are introduced: newly wed, married for more than a decade, a second marriage, and married with one child. They represent different professions, social classes, ethnic backgrounds, and ages, but all share a common challenge: the inability to have a child.

As the game show begins, the wives retreat to a soundproof booth. "Husbands, for each question you answer correctly, you will receive ten points. Question 1: Husbands, who would your wife say is to blame for your infertility?"

The camera zooms in on Husband 1. "She," he says confidently.

Husband 2: "Me. I was married before and had an operation."

Husband 3: "We don't know."

"I'm sorry, Husband 3; we cannot accept that answer. Remember this is *The Blame Game*, and we have to have someone to blame."

"I guess I'll have to say, 'The Doctor.'"

Husband 4: "God."

Of course, *The Blame Game* is not a real show, but you've probably gone through the exercise of pointing the finger at someone. Though publicly you may not blame your spouse or yourself, perhaps privately you do. Do you resent a choice you or your spouse made in the past? Are you angry because your spouse already has a child?

Did your doctor make a medical mistake, and you are living the consequences? Perhaps doctors do not know why you can't have a child. When Rich and I received this answer, we continued to do more testing even though the answer never changed. Sometimes the "not knowing" is more difficult because you want to be able to point the finger at someone.

Is God to blame for your circumstance? If you haven't suggested this answer yet, don't be surprised when you or others do. Step back and consider what Scripture says about God. He is certainly sovereign and in control. He is also a God of compassion and mercy. Satan did not slip your situation by God. Nothing in life happens without God's knowledge and permission.

Most audiences in the game show of life do not applaud when they hear this truth. Though I don't understand why disasters happen, why God allows innocent people to be killed, or a child is abused when a loving couple longs to have a child, I still know God is good. My understanding is limited. I do not have God's big picture outlook.

What's behind the blame game? I propose it is our need to feel in control. If we can point our finger at *someone*, we can make sense of something that makes no sense.

When I'm tempted to blame myself or others for my circumstances, I turn to the Old Testament story of Job. God allows Job to lose his family, his possessions, and his health. Job's friends point the finger at Job and rationalize he must have sinned. But Job's sin isn't the reason. Job's wife blames God and urges him to curse God and die. He refuses.

God finally does meet Job in his questioning. Job 38–41 recounts God's long answer to Job, which challenges Job's need for control: "Where were you when I laid the earth's foundation...." At the end of God's speech, what does Job answer? "Surely I spoke of things I did not understand, things too wonderful for me to know" (Job 42:3). And by the end of chapter 42, Job prays for a blessing on the friends who have caused him pain. What's more, Job *knows* he has been blessed of God.

If you're struggling with the blame game, I suggest you take a breath, step back, and for one moment (or one day) choose to bless—yourself, your husband, your doctor, your God—rather than blame.

Lord, help me deal with the control issue that fuels my need to blame someone for my childlessness. Forgive me. I don't understand why you have allowed my circumstance and why you are not allowing me to have a child, but I know that you are good. You are sovereign. You are wise, compassionate, and merciful. Be my comforter in my questions. Help me look beyond my questions and blame to you and to your blessing. Amen.

Steps toward Growth

1. Whom do you blame for your circumstance? Why?
2. Read Job 42. Highlight or underline meaningful sections that speak to you.
3. In Job 42:10, Job prays for those who caused him pain. Why do you think this was a turning point in his life?
4. Write a short prayer, asking God to bless those who have caused you pain.
5. Point your finger upward today. Honor and praise God as sovereign.

MY PERSONAL JOURNEY

Devotion 7

A Second Opinion?

[Jesus said,] "And I will ask the Father, and he will give you another Counselor to be with you forever—the Spirit of truth."

John 14:16–17a

What about donor sperm, donor eggs, donor embryos, frozen embryos, surrogate mothering, adoption, and foster care? If you are considering these options or others, I suggest you look at each option in light of two other questions. What is your spouse's opinion? And what is God's opinion?

Let me encourage you to talk openly with your spouse and together search for God's truth in light of Scripture. I have listed organizations and resources in the back of my book that can help you sift your options through God's viewpoint. I particularly recommend *The Infertility Companion*, written by Sandra Glahn and William Cutrer.

Perhaps you and your spouse are so desperate or driven to have a child that you are willing to ignore God's truth. Please reconsider your decision before you press on. Remember, human ways and your doctor's ways are not always compatible with God's.

As you search for God's truth and his will for you, ask yourself questions such as these:

- Can you say with certainty when God says life begins?
- What risks could you encounter when you agree to conceive or raise another person's child?

- How will this decision affect your relationship with your spouse?
  With others?
- How will you eventually share with your child how he or she
  came into being?
- Are you equipped to handle this situation at this time?

Even if it seems that God's Word approves of a certain option, you and your spouse still may not feel comfortable proceeding in that direction. That's okay. Knowing what you are *not* willing to do can help you more clearly define what you *are* willing to do.

Children are a gift from God, and I believe God has different plans to bring children into a person's life. Perhaps God has called you to birth a child "in your heart" and will deliver your child through adoption or foster care. Could he be allowing you to continue to wrestle with gray-area questions even after you've sought his truth and godly counsel because now is not his timing?

Is there a clear-cut answer to your situation? Sometimes, but not always! When you seek God's truth wholeheartedly and invite his Spirit of truth to guide you to Scripture, people, and resources to enlighten you, take good notes! God does have a purpose and plan. Are you willing to wait for God's best for your life? If you sense that he is telling you to "go for it" today, what is holding you back?

Ultimately, you and your spouse will stand face to face with your Creator and be held accountable for the decisions you made. Are you missing an opportunity today to glorify him through your decision? Do you feel as if your resistance to move ahead is due to your pride or fear, or because you sense your decision is contrary to God's truth? Do you sense God's peace and have you confirmed it in his Word?

Pour out your heart to God about the options before you and the questions you have about each one. Allow him to feed you with his Word and to lead you to others who can help you in your quest.

Lord, there are so many options to consider. I am overwhelmed by the choices I need to make. What is your plan for us to have a child? I only want what you want. Reveal your truth and lead me to those who can answer my questions from your perspective. Change my perspective to your perspective. Hug me with your peace. Amen.

STEPS TOWARD GROWTH

1. Ask the Spirit of truth (John 14:17) to help you clarify the options you are facing. What questions do you have? Write them out. Ask God to guide you to his truth and perspective. Listen. Record what comes to mind.
2. What Scriptures, organizations, or other resources point you to God's viewpoint about each option?
3. Think over your life. Remember and record the ways God has revealed his truth to you about other decisions, even those related to your journey to have a child.

MY PERSONAL JOURNEY

_____

_____

_____

_____

_____

_____

_____

_____

_____

_____

WHAT IF MY SPOUSE AND I DISAGREE?

Be kind and compassionate to one another, forgiving each other, just as Christ forgave you.

Ephesians 4:32

Rich and I have very different temperaments. His cautious, methodical-minded personality frequently clashes with my impulsive, spontaneous nature. Believe me, nothing about the experience of infertility changed my husband's basic personality. Nor mine.

I naively expected Rich always to see my point of view and agree with me. When he didn't, I interpreted his disapproval to mean "I don't care" or "I don't want a child as much as you." At times I pressured him and couldn't understand why the more I persisted, the more he resisted. (Did I ever utter the forbidden line, "If you really loved me, you would do this"? Yeow! I hope not.) My salesperson persuasive personality would kick into high gear. Although I did my best to diffuse his objections, I ultimately didn't feel God's peace. I'm embarrassed to admit that I did and said things to him that I wish I could erase. I am grateful that he is a patient and forgiving husband.

Maybe you have the perfect household, but ... I expect not. Sooner or later, you and your spouse will disagree about some aspect of your quest for a child. Your spouse may want to continue; you may want to quit. Your spouse may see only obstacles; you see opportunities. You may view the process as a financial investment; your spouse sees debt. Perhaps your spouse views "medical procedures" as "playing God"; you see them as God's answer to your prayers. Whatever the issue ... be prepared. You may not always agree.

Ultimately, I've learned that Rich's and my personalities balance our relationship and viewpoints. He tempers my impulsiveness. I prompt him to action. Although two views may cause unwanted conflict, when we choose to listen to each other lovingly, with open hearts, we enlarge our perspectives. Rich and I have come to a place where we give each other permission to share honestly without being interrupted and interrogated. We usually take time to think about what was said before we talk about it further. Then we clarify what we thought we heard.

We have experienced the power of praying and asking God to open our hearts to hear him and the other person. And if we reach an impasse, we wait. We wait on God to change the situation or our view. Sometimes we track down additional information.

As you press on, stay in step with each other. Embrace your God-given differences. Gary Chapman's book *The Five Love Languages* encouraged us to identify what method of communication best opens our heart. Because Rich's primary love language is "physical touch" and mine is "quality time," we came up with a creative solution. We met in our bedroom each night; I gave Rich a back rub, while he listened to me talk. (I had *lots* to talk about.) Rich listened as long as I massaged.

Invite God to enlarge your perspective and communication. Be creative. Thank God for your spouse's unique qualities.

Lord, thank you for creating my spouse and me as unique beings. Though at times I don't like to hear what he has to say, help me to listen with an open heart and mind. Give me patience. Enable me to forgive and to ask for forgiveness. Bring to mind anything I've done or said to my spouse for which I need to seek his forgiveness. Keep our marriage strong and help us to seek you first in all things. Amen.

Steps toward Growth

1. How do you and your spouse view the infertility experience differently?
2. What has been the greatest area of conflict in your journey? How did you overcome it? Is there anything today for which you need to seek forgiveness from your spouse? If so, do it now!
3. What unique qualities do you appreciate about your spouse? How has your spouse enlarged your perspective?
4. How could you communicate differently so that your spouse will be more open and hear you?
5. Set a time every day this week to pray together with your spouse, asking God to strengthen your marriage and to give you wisdom.

My Personal Journey

_____

_____

_____

_____

_____

_____

_____

_____

_____

_____

_____

_____

_____

"MOMMY, WILL I EVER HAVE A BROTHER OR SISTER?"

If any of you lacks wisdom, you should ask God, who gives generously to all without finding fault, and it will be given to you.

James 1:5 (TNIV)

"Mommy, will I ever have a brother or sister?" four-year-old Jennie asked as she curled up on her mother's lap. Emily and her husband Bob adored their daughter and had planned to have a second child by now. But life wasn't happening according to their plans. Conceiving Jennie had happened quickly so they assumed conceiving a second child would happen easily too. But month after month they waited. When they sought their doctor's advice, they discovered that Emily needed surgery for a blocked fallopian tube and endometriosis. During their journey a well-meaning comment, "At least you have a child," seemed to minimize their pain.

Thousands of couples understand the frustrating journey of secondary infertility: the inability to conceive or carry a child to term after successfully having a child. Their pain is often misunderstood or minimized by others. Sometimes couples themselves wonder if their longing is justifiable and feel guilty for wanting "more." Couples may hide their heartache, because they do not want their only child to feel unloved, as if he is "not enough." Or couples may feel more pain and pressure if the child keeps reminding them how much she wants a brother or sister and continually asks questions.

Perhaps you can relate to the exasperating family journey of secondary infertility. You long for a sibling for your child and want him to have a playmate and lifelong friend. Or maybe your child is grown and you are grieving the additional child you longed for but never had. You grieve the loss of someone who never was. *Is that normal,* you wonder, *especially after so many years?*

Your journey is personal and can't be compared to others. Longing for a child and the emotions that emerge at various stages in your journey is similar to grieving. On some days you may feel angry, resentful, and sad and continue to question "why?" On other days you may be at peace and accept your circumstances. Maybe today you are at a crossroads in your quest and wonder if you're just a step away from the right path that will lead you to the child you desire.

Regardless of where you are, God is there. He understands what it's like to have an only child. Pour out your heart to him today, and encourage your spouse and child to do the same. He is the answer and the only way to get through this journey. He understands what you are going through and will give you the wisdom you need so desperately. The following suggestions may help you encourage a child who longs for a brother or sister.

Be honest. Don't make promises that can't be fulfilled. If your child asks, "Will I ever have a brother or sister?" it's okay to tell him that you don't know and you hope so, but it's God's decision.

Validate your child's feelings. Children need to know that it's okay to feel sad or glad about wanting a brother or sister. Encourage her to share her feelings with you and with God.

Explore your child's needs. Why does he want a brother or sister? Perhaps he wants a playmate, friend, roommate, or someone younger so he can be "big," or maybe he sees other friends or cousins with siblings. You may be able to fulfill his need in other ways or introduce him to other children who are only children.

Give her a doll, stuffed animal, or pet to love! Although this will not take the place of a brother or sister, it can help. When Jake asked, "Mommy since all of our babies die, could I please have a puppy?" I gave in!

Volunteer to babysit a younger child. Think of a younger child in the neighborhood, family, or church nursery and offer to take care of her for an afternoon. Have your child help and talk about how much work it is!

Sponsor a child. Choose a younger child through World Vision, Angel Tree Ministries, or a local outreach in your community to help. Involve your child in the process of giving and praying for this child.

Lord, will I ever have another child? I'm grateful for _____, but I long to have another child. How can pain be so strong after I already have a baby? I don't understand.

Should I let go or press on? Help me forgive others for words they've said that have hurt me. Give me patience to respond to my child's questions and help her—and me—look to you. Amen.

STEPS TOWARD GROWTH

1. Identify the family of your dreams. How many children? Age span? Lay this dream before God. What do you sense God is saying in response to your dream?
2. How have you experienced others minimizing or misunderstanding your pain? What might be a wise and measured response to their comments?
3. Considering your own personality and that of your child, how might you effectively respond to your child's questions?
4. What do you sense God is saying to you today?

MY PERSONAL JOURNEY

_____

_____

_____

MY PERSONAL JOURNEY

_____

_____

_____

_____

_____

_____

_____

_____

_____

_____

_____

_____

_____

_____

_____

_____

_____

_____

_____

_____

_____

_____

_____

_____

_____

Devotion 10

WHAT DO YOU THINK
GOD WANTS YOU TO DO?

[Jesus] said, "Throw your net on the right side of the boat and you will find some." When they did, they were unable to haul the net in because of the large number of fish.

John 21:6

I was surprised when Dee called me to discuss her fertility challenges. As a successful businesswoman, Dee's picture appeared frequently in the paper. I had talked to her only briefly at the Christian luncheon meetings we both attended. I hadn't penetrated her confident, to-the-point persona. Frankly, I never felt we "clicked" and wondered if she even liked me.

"Thanks for meeting me," Dee said as she led the way to a corner table and ordered two cups of coffee.

"I'm glad you called," I said, smiling. I could sense her discomfort. With me? With the topic? I didn't know. "So, you want to have a child?" I continued.

"YYY . . . es," Dee stammered. Then I heard her story: Desiring professional success, she had never wanted children of her own. She'd married a man with children from a previous marriage. Yet now she *did* want a child, but her husband had had a vasectomy. "My husband is willing to have the operation reversed . . . and doctors suggest in vitro . . . but we're not sure if that's what God wants."

I hesitated. Giving advice is risky; I never want to say anything contrary to God's Word. Every journey to have a child is personal and may involve different moral choices. *God, give me wisdom and your words!* I prayed silently.

We talked about God's desire for love and unity in their marriage, her role as a stepmother, God view's of life at conception, and weighing God's truth against the doctor's advice. Dee had never considered the many decisions she and her husband might have to make.

Finally Dee looked me straight in the eyes and said, "So, what do you think God wants us to do?"

"Throw down your net on the other side!" I was amazed at my outburst. God reminded me of the story in John 21. The disciples had fished all night with no success. Then Jesus told them to move their nets—to the right side of the boat. When they did so, they were unable to haul in all the fish. We both chuckled when we discussed the application in her specific situation. I urged Dee to talk and pray with her husband and ask God to reveal his truth to them and the next steps to take.

Perhaps you are in a similar place as Dee, trying to discern what to do *next.* Like the disciples in the boat, you've had no success. You may be discouraged or weary. Imagine Jesus saying to you, *Move your nets. Throw them on the right side!*

How will you respond? Will you tell Jesus all the reasons why you can't, or will you simply trust him? Trusting Jesus may mean doing something opposite from what your doctor or others say. Like Dee, you may need to throw down your net of confidence and become vulnerable to trust another person with your pain or trust your spouse with your fear and uncertainty.

Have you been relying on your own strength to get you through? When you let down your net in trust, whatever your net is, you too can experience a successful catch. Your success may not result in a child, or perhaps it will. Your success may be a net bulging with faith or hope you never experienced before, or a new doctor or option, or even a friend to encourage you.

Will you trust Jesus and let down your net today? Ask him to show you how his words can be applied to your specific situation. Is he asking you to change course and do something different? Go ahead. Trust his words. Trust his strength. Trust his wisdom.

Pick up your net and throw it on the other side. Splash! Now pull it up and expect your net to be bulging . . .

Lord, I like being in control and self-reliant. I've experienced success in other areas of my life, but having a child seems impossible to me. I've worked hard and don't know what else to do. Help me trust you and others. Even when I'm tempted to trust myself, give me the courage to throw down my net on the other side and trust your Word. When I'm faced with difficult decisions, help me to have the courage to say "no" if the decisions are contrary to your Word. Help me trust you in new ways this week. Amen.

STEPS TOWARD GROWTH

1. Read the story of the disciples and Jesus in John 21:1–6. How can you relate to this story?
2. What do you think Jesus is saying to you personally when he says, "Throw down your nets on the right [opposite] side"?
3. What is God telling you about trust? What kind of support do you need, and from whom? What steps can you take this week to connect with someone who might help you cast your nets?

MY PERSONAL JOURNEY

Father, I love you and praise you.
You are King of Kings. Forgive me Lord for being
so in control. I trust you Lord. You are
trustworthy. You are faithful. Forgive me
for my selfish behavior. Open my eyes to
others needs - help me to see through
your eyes

My Personal Journey

please pour your wisdom down on us tonight.
Help us to hear what you want us to hear
Lay this on both our hearts the
direction you want us to take
We don't know what to do but our eyes
are on you.
We will wait for you Lord

WAITING

Waiting: *a period during which one waits; a pause or delay.*

My soul is in anguish.
> *How long, O LORD, how long?*

> > Psalm 6:3

Wait for the LORD;
> *be strong and take heart*
> *and wait for the LORD.*

> > Psalm 27:14

Yet the LORD longs to be gracious to you;
> *he rises to show you compassion.*
For the LORD is a God of justice.
> *Blessed are all who wait for him!*

> > Isaiah 30:18

THE AISLE OF UNCERTAINTY

There is one God and one mediator between God and human beings, Christ Jesus, himself human, who gave himself as a ransom for all people. This has now been witnessed to at the proper time.

1 Timothy 2:5–6 (TNIV)

I'll never forget one visit to the drugstore when I first identified the irony found on a familiar aisle. To my left I saw rows of feminine hygiene products and to my right, pregnancy tests. I was outraged, yet I laughed. I wanted to talk to the store manager about product placement and marketing sensitivity, but I didn't. Instead, I stood in limbo, in the middle of two product extremes, for me representing life or death, pregnant or not, yes or no, hope or dread. Did the center of the aisle represent maybe? Maybe? Is it possible to live in limbo—in the same aisle, but between two completely different outcomes?

I chose to purchase both products (a typical Type-A shopper attitude). As the cashier handed me my bag with both products tucked inside, I wasn't sure if I should celebrate or lament. Is it is possible to feel opposite emotions at the same time? Yes.

I think of Jochebed, the mother of Moses, who hid her infant in a floating basket to save him from the king's death sentence. I can only imagine the tug of war between her fear and faith. As she placed him in the basket and closed the lid, did she shed tears of sorrow or relief? As he floated on the river among the reeds, she must have experienced moments of dread sprinkled with hope.

Later, when Pharaoh's daughter rescued him and hired Jochebed to nurse him, Jochebed must have teeter-tottered between bitter and sweet emotions. Though the baby was in her care, she could not admit she was his mother. Moses, the middle man between two nations—Egypt and Israel—and two mothers. Opposite extremes: a son of royalty, a son of Hebrew slaves. A birthmother and an adopted mother. Both called by God to play a unique role in the aisle of his life.

As you wait in the aisle of uncertainty, in limbo between two outcomes, please know that you are not alone. Others have stood where you are standing. I know how frustrating not knowing can be. Give yourself permission to be where you are. Enjoy moments of hope. Dream. It's also normal to think about the opposite extreme. Bracing for loss does not show a lack of faith. Your personality may demand that you consider every possibility. That's okay.

But remember, God is with you in the aisle of your circumstances, and he understands. You can count on that with certainty. He loves you and sent his only Son, Jesus, to earth as a baby, to become the mediator between two opposite extremes, humanity and God. He stood between God's holiness and your sin and took the blame for what you and I deserved. He suffered and died an agonizing death between two thieves for your sin and mine. But he didn't stay in the middle; he conquered death after three days and offers us a place with him in heaven to live eternally.

Do you know with certainty that your eternal future is secure, or are you in limbo, wondering if you will spend eternity in heaven or in hell? Today, God wants you to know it's time to step out of the aisle of your spiritual uncertainty and invite Jesus into your life. Allow Jesus to take your hand and guide you through the rest of your journey and be your strength in weak moments. He will be your stabilizer when you teeter-totter between two extreme emotions and outcomes. Invite him into the middle of your life's muddle and accept his peace.

Lord Jesus, I'm living with uncertainty. I'm waiting and don't know what the outcome will be. Be my stabilizer. You hung on a cross in the middle, between two thieves. You died and rose again so that I might have life eternal. Come into my life, my limbo, my muddle. Give me your peace. Travel with me through the aisle of uncertainty in the drugstore of my experience. Amen.

STEPS TOWARD GROWTH

1. How do you cope (or have you coped) with uncertainty, being in limbo, in in-betweenness?
2. How does the life of Moses and Jochebed (Exodus 1:13–2:15; cf. 6:20) or of Jesus encourage you as you reflect on your uncertainty or being in the middle?
3. Brainstorm ways that suit your personality that can help you live *creatively* with the tension in the aisle of uncertainty.
4. If you are now turning to Christ for your salvation, write out what this means for you.

MY PERSONAL JOURNEY

_____

_____

_____

_____

_____

_____

_____

_____

_____

_____

_____

_____

_____

Devotion 12

WAITING ROOM: INCONVENIENCE OR OPPORTUNITY?

My times are in your hands.

Psalm 31:15a

I'm sorry, Ms. Wunnenberg, the doctor is running behind schedule," announced the receptionist.

I was fuming. Time was money to me. As an advertising sales representative for a television station, I had to see several clients a day and managed to stay on schedule, so why couldn't doctors? At that moment I considered storming out, but I knew that it would be months until I would get another appointment. I also considered billing the doctor for my wasted time, but decided to take a seat in the waiting room with the other disgruntled patients instead.

I vowed to make the most of my time, so I pretended that I was on a sales call. My marketing sense kicked in and I looked around the room to try and determine the demographic profile of the customers of this infertility clinic. The waiting room consisted of one lone man in the corner and several women, who looked to be in their twenties, thirties, or forties. Professional, homemakers, athletic, white, Hispanic, African American, and Asian women made up the mix. Though outwardly we all represented a diverse segment of the population, inwardly we were the same: fertility-challenged women (and men) waiting for a child.

I chuckled as I thought about the type of sales presentation I could make to this doctor to help him reach his target audience using my television station. Although Arbitron and Nielson did not have research available at that time for fertility-challenged waiting women, I considered the list of possible shows: *Married with Children, The Cosby Show, Oprah, The Evening News,* and *I Love Lucy.* Then I imagined the type of commercial that would appeal to the women surrounding me. Would humor, creative special effects, or a well-known celebrity as a spokesperson (one experiencing similar challenges) work best?

My mind raced with creative possibilities. Was it possible to communicate a private, painful experience in a positive way? I knew that *fast service* would not be a benefit I would promote. Moreover, quite honestly, I knew that the doctor probably didn't need more customers or the waiting would only increase. Then the winning strategy hit me . . . meet women where they are . . . . in the waiting room experience and help them make the most of it.

That's it! I thought.

I looked around and noticed what women were doing. Reading. Knitting. Writing. Doing crossword puzzles. Napping (oops, that was the man). And me? Dreaming and creating. Well, that time's paid off, because now it's in a book. Here are a few other suggestions to try the next time you find yourself in a waiting room experience.

- *Meet and encourage a stranger.* You have a common connection with the woman sitting next to you. Forget yourself and reach out to her. Ask her how long she's been waiting and who her doctor is, and then be prepared to encourage her with your words, experience, a joke, Scripture, or personal insights about your own journey.
- *Pray.* Use your time to pray for your doctor, nurses, and for those who are in the waiting room with you. Your prayers may be the only ones they receive today!
- *Journal.* Express your thoughts and feelings on paper. Write a letter to God.
- *Lift a friend or two.* I carry a variety of cards with me, and I can use waiting room time to reconnect with friends.
- *Write a love letter.* When was the last time you expressed your appreciation and passion to your spouse? Do it! Mail it or hide it in a special place.

- *Plan.* Need to plan a party, vacation, meals for the next week, a "honey-do" list for your home, wardrobe needs, holiday shopping list, or your budget? Now might be a good time.
- *Dream.* If you had no limitations, what would you like to do or become? Where do you see yourself in five years? Ten years? Twenty years? What experiences or accomplishments do you hope to achieve by then?
- *Connect with God.* Pull out your pocket-sized Bible and read about waiting, using passages such as Psalm 27:14; 40:11; 130:5; Isaiah 30:18; and 1 Thessalonians 1:10. Invite God to show you what he is teaching you through your waiting.
- *Rest.* Breathe deeply. Exhale your stress. Inhale peace. Be still and know that God is God. Close your eyes and rid your mind of any worries or anxious thoughts. Cast your cares on God, because he cares for you.

However you choose to use your waiting room time is up to you. I believe God has a plan and purpose for your time, just as he did for so many others—like Jonah in the belly of a fish, Lazarus in the tomb, and Paul in prison. Remember, you are in good company. Look around and look up! Perhaps your waiting room experience is an inconvenience that God will use for an unexpected opportunity.

> *Lord, I'm not a good wait-er. Help me make the most of my time. Turn my inconvenience into an opportunity. Teach me how to look beyond myself to others who may be waiting for encouragement. Slow me down, Lord. Show me your purpose and plans for my waiting room experience today. My time is in your hands, Lord. Use it today to glorify you! Amen.*

STEPS TOWARD GROWTH

1. Reflect on your last waiting room experience. How did you use your time?
2. Read the story of Jonah. The book of Jonah is only four chapters in the Bible. How did Jonah use his time of waiting in the belly of a fish? How can you relate? How did Jonah's "waiting room experience" change his attitude and actions?
3. Reflect on the phrase, "Time is opportunity." How does it change your thinking about waiting rooms? What unexpected opportunity could be waiting through your inconvenience?
4. Your time is in God's hands. How can you make the most of your waiting room experiences? (Review the list above and choose one or two items.)

MY PERSONAL JOURNEY

Wait for the Lord   Be strong and take heart
and wait for the Lord   Psalm 27.14

Father God forgive my impatience. Lord I want to be content where we are now → you know the desires of our heart to have a child. Father my thoughts are consumed. I surrender this to you — I place my trust on your word which says Delight yourself in the Lord and He will give you the desires of your heart

Thank you for your promises. I love you Lord. Forgive me for being so selfish. Open my eyes to those around us who need encouragement Father I strongly sensed that we would be 3 — Show us clearly your path Change both of our hearts as to be in quords & you will Break down the fears in both of us — we wait for You

PREPPING FOR MOTHERHOOD

I have no greater joy than to hear that my [spiritual] children are walking in the truth.

3 John 4

Ironically, as I was first trying to get pregnant, God allowed my fifteen-year-old brother, Doug, to live with us for a year because my mom and step-dad were in the process of a divorce. Little did I know through this experience God would allow us to spiritually oversee and influence a child and prepare our hearts for the role of parenting.

I became Doug's legal guardian so he could attend school in our state. More important, I believe God called Rich and me to become Doug's spiritual guardians for that season. When he arrived at our home, he was a self-professed agnostic. A typical testosterone-driven teenager, Doug challenged us to the limits, but we continued to intercede on his behalf.

We persuaded him to go to a Christian camp for a week. Reluctantly, he boarded a bus full of strangers. Burdened by my brother's unbelief and dark eternal future, I cried out to God on his behalf; I expected God to change his heart. My well-meaning, analytical husband cautioned me not to get my hopes up. Even so, I labored on my knees for my brother's spiritual birth.

When the bus finally pulled into the church parking lot a week later, a tall, lanky teenager bounded off the bus sporting a new T-shirt with God words all over it. "Hey, sis!" he shouted before hugging his new friends. A few days later I watched Doug publicly profess his faith in Jesus Christ through his baptism. I stood in awe of God's faithfulness to be my Deliverer.

In a sense, my brother became a babe whom I was privileged to nurture for a short season as a spiritual mom. When he left unexpectedly to return home, I mourned his loss. Some nights I lay prostrate on the floor and wept uncontrollably. I grieved the loss of this child who had grown *in* my heart, and a few weeks later I grieved the loss of a child who had grown *under* my heart through miscarriage.

At this point of your journey, are you so consumed with the future—waiting for fulfillment—that you aren't seeing opportunities to help birth and raise spiritual children? Yes, it might be painful to see them leave your care, but, believe me, any children born into your family will not remain babies forever. They will ultimately grow independent of you.

The apostle Paul may have had no children of his own. The Bible never mentions his natural family, and yet he addresses two letters to a young man named Timothy, his "true son in the faith" (1 Timothy 1:2) and his "dear son" (2 Timothy 1:2). Timothy was influenced by his natural mother and grandmother, but Paul claimed a part in Timothy's sharing the family name of Christ—being a Christian.

As you wait for a child of your own, don't lose sight of today. What experiences may God be using to prepare your and your spouse's hearts for delayed deliveries? There may be a teenager or a younger child in need of a seasonal spiritual guardian, or a baby in need of a lifelong intercessor. Perhaps God is preparing the soil of your heart through your circumstances to recognize and respond to your divine calling.

Lord, forgive me for being so preoccupied with my future hopes that I'm tempted to ignore the needs of others, especially the younger generation that is growing up around me. How are you preparing me now for my future? What spiritual children do you have for me to nurture—as I wait for a child of my own? I pray this in Jesus' name. Amen.

STEPS TOWARD GROWTH

1. What circumstances in your life may God be using to water and reveal your calling?
2. Read 1 Timothy 1:1–2. When Paul says, "To Timothy, my true son in the faith," how does that encourage you to think differently about parenthood?
3. God calls us to carry on his name to others. List the people whom you have influenced spiritually. Invite God to bring to mind others who may need to know Jesus.
4. Consider making a "spiritual family album," in which you can place pictures of those who have influenced you and those who have become Christians through your influence.

MY PERSONAL JOURNEY

THE MOM WITH THE GRANDMOTHER FACE

But if we hope for what we do not yet have, we wait for it patiently.

Roman 8:25

How silly to believe that I will ever be a mother and nurse a child. My sagging breasts are dry. My face is wrinkled, my eyes are blurry, my hair is grey. Why would God choose me, an old woman, to become the mother of nations? Is this his idea of a cruel joke to have a child at my age? I wonder what Abraham's wife, Sarah, thought in the years before she became pregnant. Genesis 18:12 tells us what she did when godly visitors told her she would indeed have a child in her old age: "Sarah laughed to herself as she thought, 'After I am worn out and my master is old, will I now have this pleasure?'" Yes, Sarah laughed in disbelief. Scripture tells us she laughed again a year later, for joy, seeing herself as the mom—a mom with the grandmother face.

Did Sarah ponder how her age would impact her child? Did she imagine herself taking her child to his first day of school with all of the other 'young' mothers? Mistaken as the grandmother, she would always wear the stigma of old age. Would she be able physically to endure chasing after her toddler? And how would her child feel about her when he gazed into her creviced, spotted face? How would he respond when she told him *she* had to take a nap and change *her* diaper? Would his eyes dim with disappointment? Would he long for a different mom?

I've talked to and gleaned insights from many women who waited for years to become mothers. Older moms face numerous health challenges; odds increase for birth defects and miscarriage. Infant and toddler care, including sleep deprivation, test one's physical stamina.

I know—having had two babies myself after turning forty. Many of my friends were empty nesters. Some were even grandmothers. Though I'm not as old as Sarah was, I can relate to some of what she must have experienced in her waiting and in her role as an older mom.

Though I jest about wearing a T-shirt that says, "I'm the mom, not the grandmother," deep down I know this is a painful truth I must face. I will probably be the oldest mom picking up my younger two (but hopefully the wisest!) from school. I may never experience being a grandmother.

Sarah's willingness to become "a mom with a grandmother face" inspires me to press on. I don't understand why God allowed me to wait this long to become a mom again, but he did. Instead of a season of freedom, I am fatigued. My back goes out more than I do. Should I buy Pampers *and* Depends? Is it worth it? Absolutely! God has a plan for my life, and he has one for yours too, with or without children.

Perhaps you are at a place in your journey where you are questioning if you're too old to keep trying to have a child. Yes, there certainly are risks and challenges, and I would encourage you and your spouse to consider them carefully with your doctor and invite others to pray with you and for you. Are you tired of waiting for a biological child? Could God be calling you to consider other options? Waiting can be frustrating and cause you to question and doubt. That's normal.

As you wait, remember to look up into the starlit sky to your Creator. Ask him to sustain you and to reveal his purpose for your longings to be fulfilled. He will help you endure your waiting. He sustained Sarah, and he sustained me. And should you become a "mom with a grandmother face," he will give you the strength and courage to fulfill that role too.

Lord, how long must I wait? My biological clock is ticking. What are your plans to fulfill my longing for a child? You are my Creator, and you gave me the desire for a child. Please fulfill my longing or lessen my desire. Give me wisdom as I wait. Replace my frustration with options to consider. Whatever you decide, even if you desire me to become an older mom, I am willing to accept that. I will wait on you. Amen.

STEPS TOWARD GROWTH

1. Reflect on Sarah's life. How can you relate to her as you wait?
2. How long are you willing to wait for a child?
3. What unique circumstances do you think "older parents" encounter? Discuss this with your spouse. What risks are you willing to accept? Talk with your doctor. What is your doctor's advice? What other options might you consider?
4. What is God teaching you through your waiting?

MY PERSONAL JOURNEY

_____

_____

_____

_____

_____

_____

_____

_____

_____

Devotion 15
WAITING TO CROSS OVER

*Go through the camp and tell the people, "Get your supplies
ready. Three days from now you will cross the Jordan here to
go in and take possession of the land the LORD your God is
giving you for your own."*

Joshua 1:11

"Get ready to cross over!"

Imagine with me the celebration of the Israelites camped at the banks of
the Jordan with their final destination in view, hearing those words. After forty
years of waiting, their dream was about to become reality. "We made it!" Their
perseverance had paid off, though many times they had doubted and wondered
if they could make it another step. Victory was just a river crossing away. With
no ferries in sight, did they ponder if they should swim across? How would they
get to the other side?

Before they could respond, the command came for all twelve tribes to get
in line and follow the ark of the covenant. As the ark was carried across the Jordan River, God caused the water at flood stage to recede, allowing all the people
to walk across on dry land. What a majestic ending and a new beginning! The
Deliverer, God himself, led the procession into a new land with new (sometimes fearsome) challenges.

Our crossing-over moment came when the adoption agency called and said,
"Your son has been born!" Rich and I were ecstatic. Think hugs, high fives, and
"hurrays." After a miscarriage, several years in the desert of infertility, and a failed
adoption, the promised land of parenthood had always seemed unreachable. A

few days later after the birth parents signed release forms, we drove to pick up our son. I looked at the empty car seat and wondered how it would feel to finally fill it. I had waited so long and persevered, yet I still questioned whether or not I could live up to the role of being a mom.

"God, help me!" I whispered. Peace enveloped me, and I knew that allowing God to lead our parenthood procession would be the only way we would be able to make it in a new role. My Deliverer had delivered and would help me cross over.

Sooner or later your journey through infertility may lead you to a place of crossing over to parenthood. Like the Israelites after years of waiting, you may hear the words, "You're pregnant," or "You're in labor," or "You've been matched." You may celebrate, even as you are overwhelmed with emotion and questions.

Becoming a parent is the beginning of another lifelong journey, one that opens the doors to different longings: for your child to know God, for you to nurture your child and help him grow, for you to be the best parent you can be. As you cross over, allow your Deliverer to lead your procession—all the way to the eternal Promised Land.

Regardless of where you are in your waiting journey, God's desire is that you look to him and allow him to lead you. The apostle Paul says, "I tell you, now is the time of God's favor, now is the day of salvation" (2 Corinthians 6:2). What does it mean for you to let him to be your Deliverer today?

Lord, I know that you want to bless me—deliver me—today, even as I wait for the grand crossing over into your heavenly home, the ultimate Promised Land. Please lead me through any number of smaller "crossings" along the way. You are my Lord, my Savior, my Deliverer. In you will I trust. Amen.

STEPS TOWARD GROWTH

1. Read the story of preparing to cross the Jordan (Joshua 1) and the actual crossing over (Joshua 3) as if God is speaking to you personally. Underline phrases that encourage you.

2. There are many "crossing over" times in your journey to have a child. Perhaps you've crossed over to pursue professional medical support, counseling, or adoption. Reflect on those moments.
3. Name the next crossing that you are hoping to make.
4. Take a moment to talk to God and celebrate the crossing(s) that he has enabled you to make. Invite him to lead your procession as you persevere.

My Personal Journey

_____

_____

_____

_____

_____

_____

_____

_____

_____

_____

_____

_____

_____

_____

RESENTING

Resenting: *to feel or show displeasure or indignation*
at from a sense of injury or insult.

Deliver me from my enemies, O God;
    protect me from those who rise up against me.

                      Psalm 59:1

But as for me, my feet had almost slipped;
    I had nearly lost my foothold.
For I envied the arrogant
    when I saw the prosperity of the wicked.
They have no struggles;
    their bodies are healthy and strong.

                   Psalm 73:2–4

WHINING IN THE WILDERNESS

Pray continually; give thanks in all circumstances, for this is God's will for you in Christ Jesus.

1 Thessalonians 5:17–18

I don't like being *told* what to do!" I groaned. "I wish we could be like 'normal couples,' whose plans turn out the way they want."

Perhaps you, too, have uttered these words.

When the construction management company where Rich worked announced we would be transferred from Oregon to Arizona, we were unprepared for this news. We were confident that Texas would be our new home and had already taken a trip there (at our expense), reconnected with friends, and investigated housing. I had even interviewed for jobs. Living in the Sonoran Desert had never been part of our plans.

The week in April 1983 when Rich and I reluctantly moved from chilly, misty Oregon to Arizona, temperatures soared to record-breaking triple digits. As we sped toward our destination through the desolate desert, our Z–28 Camaro overheated. We were forced to turn off the air conditioner and roll down the windows. Hot, blustery air filled the sports car. I noticed all of my plants in the backseat of our car were drooping from the intense heat.

"Rich, why did you tell your company we would move?" I whined as I wiped the perspiration from my brow. Rich rolled his eyes at me. Silence pervaded the car. My husband knew words would not fix the situation.

"I loved my job in sales at the television station! I doubt if I'll ever find another one like it," I whimpered.

Again my husband's wisdom in silence prevailed.

"Let's turn around and go back," I sniveled. But my husband continued to drive to Phoenix.

At times in your journey to have a child, you may be tempted to fuss and whine. Like the Israelites in the wilderness who mumbled and complained about eating the same food every day—the mysterious manna; the word itself means "what is it?"—and wanted to return to Egypt, you may resent your current condition. You may look back, remember the way things used to be, and grumble.

I can understand that on a bad day one spouse may need to vent feelings. What may appear as whining may really be a necessary release. If a spouse needs to express pain or frustration, perhaps you could set a timer and say, "You can complain all you want for three minutes." Don't say anything. Just listen. Silence can be a gift you and your spouse give each other.

However, take it from a fellow whiner, after you've released your concerns, look up. Look beyond the woe-is-me self-pity that fuels discontent, complaining, and whining. As hard as it might be, the next time you find yourself feeling sorry for yourself and whining, stop and name one aspect of your day or your life that you can thank God for. It may be as basic as thanking him for central heating or air conditioning or for a comfortable bed or for your devoted pet dog.

Even in the wilderness the Israelites received daily manna from heaven. Even today he provides your spirit strength for the journey.

Lord, I'm tired of waiting and want to be done with this process. It is hard for me to give thanks in all my circumstances—even as I lay out my complaints before you. Thank you for listening. Forgive me for my self-pity. Help me to see the gifts you give me that I take for granted. Help me to see you in the midst of my wilderness of whining. Amen.

STEPS TOWARD GROWTH

1. What frustration are you facing today that you are tempted to whine about?
2. Communicate your frustration to your spouse today. Ask him to listen to you and support you with silence. Set a timer for five minutes. At the end of the five minutes name one thing you are thankful for. Reset the timer and give your spouse a turn to vent. Ask him also to include one thanksgiving to God.
3. Talk to God. Tell him what you appreciate about him. How has he revealed himself to you through your circumstance?

MY PERSONAL JOURNEY

Father God - Thank you 1st + most for your
Salvation gift - love grace + mercy   Forgive
me for whining + being so consumed that
I do not see your work at had + glorify you.
Father we are waiting in the desert for your
direction - I have a peace that you are
going to bring a baby - if we need to take
another step of faith - make it clear to us.
Open our eyes and our heart to adoption
if that is your desire for us.
Be with Ron + Kary as they pursue adoption
bring a child into their home. Be with Dolly
+ the kids. Be with each of the girls in
our class - surround them & your love + peace

Father thank you - I love you Lord. Show us
your will - Bring 83 people into our life
to speak truth

Devotion 17

MANDATORY ROMANTIC ENCOUNTERS

I belong to my lover, and his desire is for me.

Song of Songs 7:10

Solomon's and his wife's erotic, uninterrupted sexual encounters (depicted in the book of Song of Songs in the Bible) obviously did not take into account basal thermometers, temperature charts, and perfectly timed lovemaking. Oh . . . for the days of spontaneous sex, especially for fertility-challenged couples during ovulation time.

If only there were a simple lover's solution to remove the frustration fertility-challenged couples often feel when intimate lovemaking becomes performance on demand.

Unfortunately many times during the month when you *are* in the mood to make love, it's the wrong time. And when it's the right time, your emotional state registers "no way!" Ultimately you wonder, *How did we get here—to a place where we resent having sex?*

Rich didn't seem to mind timed lovemaking as much as me. Why should I be surprised? He's a guy. He's wired for lists, agendas, schedules, and no-frills sex. Most of the time he was thrilled to know we had a quota to meet. Me? I'm a hopeless romantic. I resent being told to perform. I can't just flip a switch and become a love machine. I need time to emotionally engage and build up to be receptive to Rich. Candles, conversation, and *moonlight* are a must for me.

I'm not a morning person. This was a challenge when our doctor prescribed morning love encounters. So, I got creative. Occasionally I stayed up all night, pulled down the shades in the morning, and took a personal day or half day off from work to sleep. This became a bit more challenging when I had mandatory morning sales meetings. One morning I was late because of prescribed morning romance. When my boss demanded a reason for my lateness, I told her the truth. Needless to say, she never asked again when I was late, but just gave me a knowing smile.

Fortunately my job flexibility allowed me to take extended lunch hours (without approval from my boss) when Rich and I had to rendezvous for prescribed afternoon delight. I felt a bit daring some days when I'd leave a boardroom meeting and head for the bedroom. Variety can be fun if you choose to have a positive attitude.

So how do couples survive "medical-must lovemaking" and get in the mood, even when they're not? Here are suggestions from several couples I've talked to:

- "We take turns keeping track of the monthly calendar so one of us is 'surprised.' The person who is in the know is the initiator."
- "I email my husband at work with a special secret phrase to let him know when and where."
- "I draw a smiley face with soap on our bathroom mirror."
- "I put my baseball hat on the bedpost so my wife knows 'It's game time!'"
- "I leave a romantic card in my wife's car."
- "Occasionally, we take a month off from temperature charts and pretend we're newlyweds, complete with a weekend getaway."
- "We pray together and invite God to give us good communication, passion, creativity, and humor."

When I took Clomid, I had terrible mood swings that had an adverse effect on our intimacy. If you are taking medication, talk to your doctor or pharmacist about the possible side effects—including its effect on your libido. When you're not in the mood for love and feel pressured to be, you may need to give yourself permission to take a month off from the routine. Sometimes your marriage is more important than your fertility challenge.

If possible, talk to others who are going through what you are. I highly recommend connecting with people through Hannah's Prayer Ministry at www.hannahsprayer.org, or refer to other support groups in the back section of my book.

Song of Songs is a great "I'm in the mood for love" book in the Bible to read. Consider reading to each other. God's desire is that you look to him and invite him into your bedroom and the challenges you may be facing in your love life. Your Creator knows everything about you and your spouse, including what you are feeling right now. He created the gift of sex and wants you to enjoy it to the fullest, even during this "timing" and season.

> *God, I don't like being told I have to be in the mood for love. I want to freely enjoy the gift of sex that you gave. Help me to be creative and flexible. Ignite my passion for you and for my spouse. Thank you for loving me uncondi- tionally, no matter what mood I'm in. Amen.*

STEPS TOWARD GROWTH

1. Describe how you are feeling about your love life. What is frustrating you? What do you enjoy? Picture your "ideal" romantic encounter with your spouse. Be specific. Where? When? How? What? What could enhance your romance—that is, candles, music, flowers, satin sheets, environment?
2. Review the ideas listed above. What one idea could you and your spouse try this month?
3. What verses in Song of Songs encourage you?

MY PERSONAL JOURNEY

JOURNEY TO THE FOREST FIRE

Finally, brothers, whatever is true, whatever is noble, whatever is right, whatever is pure, whatever is lovely, whatever is admirable—if anything is excellent or praiseworthy—think about such things.

Philippians 4:8

- "You can always adopt!"
- "Maybe it's for the best!"
- "It's only a miscarriage . . . at least you lost it early."
- "Be thankful at least that you have one child!"
- "Just relax . . . I bet that's the problem!"

Sound familiar? These are a few of the comments people made to us. Has anyone ever made a statement like this to you? If not, sooner or later they probably will. Well-meaning family and friends often become the know-it-alls in our life and want to make us feel better about our inability to conceive or carry a child. These words, intended to comfort us in our journey, instead minimized our feelings and intensified our longing for a child.

I'll never forget the astonished look on my husband's face the day that someone jokingly said, "Maybe you need to get a different wife!" Fortunately I left the room and restrained myself from lashing back, although every fiber in my being was blazing like a forest fire out of control. Even though the words had been said in jest, the spark of my wounded ego let the words smolder for weeks in my heart. *Hmm. If Rich had another wife . . . would* she *be able to have a child with him?*

I can only imagine how barren Sarah must have felt when she and Abraham gathered with family and friends. How did she endure the looks, the jeers, the whispers, year after year? Did someone ever joke with Abraham, "Maybe you need to get a different wife"? I've often wondered if a thoughtless comment like that could have been the spark that ignited Sarah's thought life and enflamed her suggestion to enlist the help of her maid Hagar to bear Abraham's first child (Genesis 16:1–2). Even though God had promised Sarah and Abraham a child, was Sarah so weary in her waiting that she allowed other people's comments to guide her wayward thoughts?

When others make well-meaning or supposedly humorous but utterly thoughtless comments about your childlessness, how will you respond? Will you choose to allow the hurts to fire you up, charring your attitudes and relationships? Will they smolder for months? Or will you douse them before they have a chance to burn?

Consider even how you might respond to a doctor's professional comment. If a doctor says, "You may need to consider donor eggs," will you see this option as a threat to your womanhood or your standing as wife or mother—as if your husband has another wife? Or could this be God's provision to bring about the child you long for? Be honest with yourself and with your spouse.

If you don't feel complete peace about a decision, wait. Seek more information. Ultimately try to determine why you feel the way you do. Is it based on distorted thought or on genuine concerns or convictions? Seek God and his truth and his will for you. Sometimes "deciding not to decide" for a specific time frame is the best decision to make. If Sarah and Abraham had done that, I wonder how things might be different in our world today.

On this journey, as you can see, there are many instances when we have opportunity to let a spark of emotion light a forest fire. In regard to our thought life, what does Scripture ask of us? To think about the true, the noble, the right, the pure, the lovely, the admirable—that which is "excellent or praiseworthy" (Philippians 4:8).

God does have a purpose and a plan for you and does not want to harm you; rather, he wants to give you hope and a future. Look to him. Ponder his words. What are *his* thoughts about your situation? Listen to him . . . then respond.

Dear Lord, help! My thoughts, fueled by my emotions, are blazing out of control. Extinguish any harmful fire with your truth. I need your perspective. Your love. Your forgiveness. Your steadying presence. Help me focus on the true, the noble, the right. Amen.

STEPS TOWARD GROWTH

1. What thoughtless comments that others have said to you have sparked a forest fire in your mind?
2. Write a letter to God today. Tell him who hurt you and what fiery thoughts you are trying to contain.
3. Don't continue to smolder. Ask God to reveal to you whom you need to forgive or what thoughts you need to "douse." Do it right now. Today I forgive _____ for _____.

MY PERSONAL JOURNEY

_____

_____

_____

_____

_____

_____

_____

_____

Devotion 19

ROSE OF FORGIVENESS

Father, forgive them, for they know not what they are doing.
Luke 23:34

I was on the way to my hair appointment when I sensed a strong urge to stop and buy a pink flower. Because I don't think clearly in the mornings, I dismissed the thought. But it came back. *Stop and get a pink flower.*

God, is that you? If so, why would you want me to buy a pink rose when I want a latte?

I still wasn't sure if this was my crazy thought or God's. Reluctantly, I stopped by the grocery store. It was right before Valentine's Day. Red. Red. Red. Not a pink flower in sight. I turned to leave but felt prompted to peek behind the display. I found dozens more red roses. But wait, centered in the cluster of red was a solitary pink rose, not real, like the others, but silk. I bought it and drove to my appointment.

Minutes later armed with two lattes, two muffins, and a pink rose I rushed to my hair appointment. Brenda jokingly calls herself "my hairapist." The first time we met we clicked, and over time we've become deeply connected. We share our hurts, hopes, disappointments, and dreams, but, more important, we anticipate sharing our faith experiences and praying together. Brenda's dynamic "hairapist" ministry has greatly influenced me and many other women. Anything is possible at Brenda's.

"I had to make a 'God stop' before I got here," I said as I handed her the pink rose.

Brenda's eyes misted with tears as she gently stroked the silk petals. "I can't believe this . . . a pink rose," she whispered.

My amazement mounted as she recalled her abortion years earlier and her guilt, forgiveness, and continued longing to have a child, though she remained single in her forties.

"Kathe, did you know this is Right-to-Life week?" she asked. She had attended a service where pink and blue flowers had represented the babies lost. "I've been asking God to show me in a tangible way if I should share my story with the high school girls I disciple this week."

"Well, Brenda, it looks like God answered," I said. "I think he wants you to share your story with the girls. And . . . maybe he also wants to remind you that his forgiveness lasts forever. It doesn't wilt—*silk*, get it?"

God used a simple pink rose to open my eyes to see beyond the pain of child-less couples. How often I have overlooked the silent suffering of godly, nurturing, single people like my friend Brenda, who would make a great parent.

God also reminded me of how I have judged people too harshly for past choices. Perhaps you know others who have lost a child through a personal choice and resent them because of it. You may point your finger at them, but when you do—remember, you have four fingers pointing back at yourself.

Perhaps you have wondered why God would allow children to be lost when so many hopeful, prospective parents long to have a child. Are you weary from carrying the silent burden of blame? Is it time to release your red-faced resentment toward others—or even toward God?

Could today be the day that God is whispering to you, "Father, forgive them for they know not what they have done"? *What a crazy thought*, you may think. But don't dismiss the idea too quickly. Trust me, when God speaks to your heart with truth, listen and do what he says. Release your blame. Forgive others.

Lord, at times I've resented others for making choices that you say are wrong. Forgive _____, but also forgive me for how I've responded to her. I don't understand why you don't intervene when I think you should. Forgive me for how I've blamed you. You are God. You are sovereign. You are all-knowing, and I am not. Thank you for Jesus, the perfect rose. Fill my life with the fragrance of your love, peace, and forgiveness today. Amen.

STEPS TOWARD GROWTH

1. Identify a time when you knew God spoke to you personally. (It may be a time when he spoke through Scripture, a song, a person, or a life circumstance.)

2. Read Mark 11:25; Luke 11:4; 23:34; Colossians 3:13. What does God tell you about forgiveness?

3. Try to envision how your relationship with a specific person will change as you live out your forgiveness, your release of resentment or blame.

4. If your resentment or blame is directed toward God, allow him to replace that resentment with his peace.

5. Purchase a blue or pink silk rose as a reminder that God's love is everlasting, and so is his forgiveness. Consider giving it to the person you listed above as a tangible reminder that she is forgiven.

MY PERSONAL JOURNEY

_____

_____

_____

_____

_____

My Personal Journey

_____

_____

_____

_____

_____

_____

_____

_____

_____

_____

_____

_____

_____

_____

_____

_____

_____

_____

_____

_____

_____

_____

_____

_____

DOES THE SHOE FIT?

*Finally, be strong in the Lord and in his mighty power. Put
on the full armor of God so that you can take your stand
against the devil's schemes . . . and with your feet fitted with
the readiness that comes from the gospel of peace.*

Ephesians 6:10–11, 15

C inderella is one of my favorite fairy tales. For years I identified with Cinderella. I dreamed of and married my handsome prince, but when my
storybook dreams of becoming a mom didn't come true, you might say my perspective changed. I saw myself being more like the stepsisters at the end of the
story. I tried to cram my foot into the glass shoe of motherhood, but it wasn't
working. I envied others who could wear and were wearing the shoe. Like the
stepsisters, I understood the longing to become someone I could not.

Perhaps you have hurled silent screams at another woman who is wearing
the shoe of motherhood. Will the shoe ever fit? Will you always remain on the
sidelines watching Cinderella mothers, or will you someday live the "fairy tale"
of your dreams? Maybe you can relate to this prayer of Evelyn Bence titled
"Where's My Miracle?"

My friend meant it so sincerely: "I just thank God for my miracle."
The big one. The event for which she'd be grateful to her dying day.

I smiled. And gulped. And, I'm ashamed to admit, wondered why
I'd never gotten mine.

"Rejoice with those who rejoice," wrote Paul, surely knowing that
it's easier to weep with those who weep.

Help me rejoice with her. Help me overlook her insensitivity to my oversensitivity.

And the miracle. I'm waiting, God, for my turn.

From *Prayers for Girlfriends and Sisters and Me*,
by Evelyn Bence. Used by permission of the author.

Whether or not you ever get the particular miracle you want, God has a royal shoe for you to wear. Are you ready to slip on the *shoes of peace* that the apostle Paul describes in Ephesians 6?

If you have accepted Jesus Christ, you are part of the royal family. God is your King. Christ is your Prince. And you are a princess. Start thinking of yourself that way. Dress the part. The Prince of Peace is kneeling before you, holding a glass slipper. Will you try it on? Will the shoe fit? Go ahead. No matter how ugly, smelly, or oversized your foot may be, don't worry. The spiritual shoe of peace will always fit if you'll be willing to slip it on.

Lord, will the shoe ever fit? Will I ever wear the shoe of motherhood? It seems as if I'm always watching others become Cinderella moms. Please forgive me for the times I've envied others and screamed silently. Give me the willingness to slip on your shoes of peace today. With those shoes, may I step confidently, with new assurance that I can do all things through you, who gives me strength. Thank you for the gift of eternal life—the promise of living happily ever after with you. Amen.

STEPS TOWARD GROWTH

1. With which character in the Cinderella story do you most identify? Why?

2. Try to identify the resentment you feel toward friends or family members with children by writing your own prayer titled "Where's My Miracle?"

3. Read Ephesians 6:10–17 and make this your daily dress-code prayer. Look carefully at verse 15. How can peace equip you with a "readiness" that might help you quash resentment that harms your relationships?
4. As a visual reminder to wear the shoes of peace, consider buying a glass slipper and a copy of the book Cinderella. Or write down Ephesians 6:15 and slip it into a glass frame. (This can also remind you that you will live happily ever after, eternally!)

MY PERSONAL JOURNEY

MY PERSONAL JOURNEY

_____

_____

_____

_____

_____

_____

_____

_____

_____

_____

_____

_____

_____

_____

_____

_____

_____

_____

_____

_____

_____

_____

_____

HOPING

Hoping: *to look forward to with desire and reasonable confidence.*

Be joyful in hope, patient in affliction, faithful in prayer.

Romans 12:12

. . . but those who hope in the LORD
will renew their strength.
They will soar on wings like eagles;
they will run and not grow weary,
they will walk and not be faint.

Isaiah 40:31

We have this hope as an anchor for the soul, firm and secure.

Hebrews 6:19

MARATHON MOTHER

Do you not know that in a race all the runners run, but only one gets the prize? Run in such a way as to get the prize. Everyone who competes in the games goes into strict training. They do it to get a crown that will not last; but we do it to get a crown that will last forever.

1 Corinthians 9:24–25

In high school, I ran track. As a newlywed, I moved to Eugene, Oregon, known as the runner's capital of the world. When I worked at a radio station near a popular running trail, I got an occasional glance at history makers Alberto Salazer and Mary Decker Tabb.

Though I had minimal exposure to long-distance running, I decided to give it a try. I looked great at the starting point, clad in my Gortex running wear and designer shoes. But by the end of the trail, I was a breathless, mud-spattered mess. I quickly wondered what inspired long-distance runners to keep running. Were blistered feet, blackened toe nails, and pulled muscles their motivators, or was perseverance the payoff? I didn't stay with the sport. But sometimes I wonder if I had stuck to it and persevered beyond the pain, would I ever have made it to the finish line of a marathon?

Your journey to have a child is similar to running a marathon. Inspired and hopeful, you gear up. At the starting line you may look and feel great, but a year or two later your energy fades, and you are a breathless mess. Disillusioned and discouraged, you wonder if you should quit or press on. Perhaps you run on, but have a temporary setback from a pulled medical or monetary muscle.

You stop to heal and regroup, then continue. Spectators cheer, "You can do it!" Driven and inspired by the vision of your prize at the finish line, you jog on even though you don't know how long it will take for you to get there.

You notice runners along the sidelines who have quit the race. Perhaps they are fatigued physically, emotionally, or financially, dehydrated from doubt or blistered with unbelief.

You are tempted to stop and join them, but two runners, Hope and Faith, pace beside you. "Keep running! Persevere!" they shout. You sense a supernatural power in your step, an unexplained confidence in your stride as you run with this duo. Your companions encourage you to stay in the race, keeping you focused on the prize. Perhaps the end is just around the next bend. Your prize is waiting for you. Run on. Run on. Run on.

You round the corner. A crowd lines the trail leading to the banner flanked with pink and blue balloons. You hear claps, shouts, whistles. Just a few more steps to victory, where you will receive your prize. Congratulations, Marathon Mother.

Lord, help me run the race to have a child. Help me stay focused on the prize and not on the pain. Give me the power to endure and the wisdom to know when to stop, regroup, or press on. When I am dehydrated with doubt and blistered with unbelief, bring companions of Hope and Faith to run with me and encourage me.

Enable me to run in your strength and not depend on myself. Refuel me with your Word of truth and discernment. Help me persevere. Don't allow me to become discouraged if I see others drop out of the race. Even if the prize for me looks different from what I had envisioned, help me sense your victory in my stride. Today, help me run my race as if I'm getting the prize. Amen.

STEPS TOWARD GROWTH

1. Where are you in the marathon to have a child? Early in the race, midway, injured and healing on the sidelines, near the end, at the finish line, or out of the race?

2. Name the running companions who encourage you with hope and faith to stay focused on the finish line. Express your appreciation to them—today. If you do not have people to encourage you, ask God to bring to mind someone who can come alongside you. Contact that person today.

3. What "prize" does Paul speak about in 1 Corinthians 9:24? How does this encourage you to respond as you run your race to have a child?

4. Perhaps you will achieve victory and become a Marathon Mother, or maybe not. Regardless of the outcome of your personal race, how can you allow God to use your experience and training to come alongside other marathoners who are early in the race?

5. Whom do you know who may need hope and faith today? How could you encourage them today? Go run—encourage this person today!

MY PERSONAL JOURNEY

_____

_____

_____

_____

_____

My Personal Journey

_____

_____

_____

_____

_____

_____

_____

_____

_____

_____

_____

_____

_____

_____

_____

_____

_____

_____

_____

_____

_____

_____

_____

_____

MAYBE TODAY

*Therefore we do not lose heart. Thought outwardly we are
wasting away, yet inwardly we are being renewed day by day.*
2 Corinthians 4:16

The sunrise of another cycle begins. Morning rays of hopefulness shine
through my clouds of disappointment. Today is a new day. The bird
perched deep within my soul sings a wordless melody of expectation. *Perhaps
today is the day a new life will be conceived.* A gentle breeze of optimism whispers to my heart. *Maybe today...*

The flowers of faith begin to bloom in the meadow of my mind. Their
sweet fragrance makes me smile. A bouquet of new beginnings beckons my
name. *Today. Perhaps today.*

The warmth of wonder guides me along the tree-lined pathway of possibilities—lush, green, tall. What is beyond the bend of uncertainty? Hand in
hand with confidence, I trek onward. Following the spirit of adventure I round
the corner. *Today? Is today the day?*

A rainbow of color welcomes me. Purple grey mountains rise up from the
sparkling river of blue-green water. A blanket of red, yellow, and pink roses covers the ground. An endless turquoise sky sprinkled with puffs of white covers the
canvas of creation. Life is everywhere. In awe of its beauty I embrace the lover
of my soul and surrender myself. Two hearts beat as one in the garden of promise beneath the midday sun. *Yes! Today!*

The warmth of afternoon sunlight surrounds me. Together I eagerly anticipate "life" with my Creator. I dream. I hope. I trust. *"And God said, be fruitful
and multiply...."*

Only time will tell. I cling to the light of the moment and pray that night's darkness never arrives. Will the sun fade into the horizon, or will it stay shining and illuminate the womb of my waiting? *Only my Creator knows.*

God is the author and giver of life. Look to him today. Bask in his presence. Look around. Let his light reveal all he has made in nature. See his signature all around you. Be still and know that he is God. He is everywhere. He is light. He is life. He created today for you to enjoy. His creation shouts, "Live life to the fullest!" Don't allow the shadows of doubt and distraction to rob you of today. Embrace your Creator. Live today! And even if the sun sets on your desire, his light of love will never fade.

Lord, is today the day? Will we create life? Only you know. Help us to embrace today and live. Enable us to bask in your presence and enjoy all you have created for us and one another. Color our lives with hope and trust. Put a new song in our soul. Thank you for the miracle of creation. Help us wait expectantly in the light of your love. Amen.

STEPS TOWARD GROWTH

1. Read Genesis 1. Look to God as your Creator. What do you appreciate about your surroundings today?
2. In what nature settings do you feel closest to God? (ocean, mountains, etc.)
3. Consider inviting your spouse to join you on an outdoor outing. Get up and watch the sunrise. Take a walk. Sit by a lake. Pick wild flowers. Cuddle next to a campfire. Enjoy creation and allow it to be the natural setting as you hope to create life.

MY PERSONAL JOURNEY

Father I praise you for being King of Kings
creator of all things. You are the author
and giver of life. Thank you for your love,
grace + mercy. Forgive me for being selfish
and shortsighted and for trying to be in control
I pray + lift up Jim + Brenda + the Bourthrop
family - Surround them with your peace, heal them
Megan. Keep her safe, help her to proclaim you - pain
Karen . give her direction + wisdom
Jessie - help her to make good decisions — move
out of her boyfriends condo
Protect both our parents. Help Jesse to
abound at work — Calm everyones spirit
Father you are in control of our baby
you know how he will come to us
I pray for a healthy baby, healthy
pregnancy forgive me for my unbelief
make our path clear   We will be
Still and know that You are God
We also know the you desire to give us
the desires of our heart - If it is yourself
Thank you for being our provider

HOPE AND JOY

This is the day the LORD has made;
let us rejoice and be glad in it.

Psalm 118:24

"You're pregnant!" my doctor announced with a smile.

My response? Silence. Though this should have been a celebratory moment for me, it wasn't. I was scared. *Will I lose this child too?* I wondered. I couldn't bear the thought of losing a fifth child. So I quelled my excitement. I tempered my hope so I would not be disappointed again. I vowed not to tell others about my pregnancy until I was further along. I refused to dream, to enjoy, to think about my child until my sixteen-week ultrasound. I felt as if hope was my enemy.

Hope could not be trusted. It had betrayed me in the past. Of course I *wanted* to be excited, but . . . I fought hard to divert the arrows of anticipation. I refused to yield to the surprise attacks of joy that tried to infiltrate my barriers. Geared with skepticism and reluctance, I would not allow hope to deceive me again.

Fighting hope is normal when you've been disappointed. Are you afraid to unleash your emotions and give yourself permission to celebrate? God understands exactly what you are feeling today. He understands your past disappointments and knows how afraid you are to envision a success.

I find a wonderful story in the book of Nehemiah. The Jewish people have been in exile in Babylon for years. But they've returned home. They've labored and labored to rebuild the walls of Jerusalem, their home. Now the wall is finished, and the people have gathered for a ceremonious reading of the Scriptures. They've longed for this day for decades. They're tired.

They've come to a milestone. The wall is built, though not yet dedicated. They are happy to be alive, but they've lost loved ones on this journey. They've come to a breakthrough moment, but they don't know what more challenges lie ahead of them. On this day, how do they respond, and what does Nehemiah say to them?

> "Do not mourn or weep." For all the people had been weeping as they listened to the words of the Law.
>
> Nehemiah said, "Go and enjoy choice food and sweet drinks, and send some to those who have nothing prepared. This day is sacred to our Lord. Do not grieve, for the joy of the LORD is your strength."
>
> Nehemiah 8:9–10

Do you see what I see? They were to celebrate the moment. Why? Because this day was sacred. (Isn't every day?) How? As they were strengthened in and by the joy of the Lord.

If and when you receive good news—any good news—give yourself permission to celebrate, maybe not publicly but quietly with your spouse and in your spirit. Allow yourself to feel the joy of this moment. I needed to learn this lesson myself. Refuse to be robbed of this day's excitement, not because this day's good fortune may be your ultimate good news, but because this day itself is the day the Lord has made. Rejoice and be glad in its gift—because he gives you the strength of his joy.

Embrace hope. Trust God and live life to the full today! In hope, with the God of hope.

Lord, I feel as if hope is my enemy. My past disappointments and my future fears are stealing my joy. The battle within my soul rages on. Help me, Lord! Help me to see that you are the joy that gives me strength—strength to celebrate a small, or large, victory. You are my Hope. I surrender my disappointments and fears to you today. Fill me with faith, hope, and love. Today, I choose to trust you and hope again. Thank you, Lord! Amen.

STEPS TOWARD GROWTH

1. How and when do you feel that hope is your enemy?
2. What past disappointments are robbing your joy?
3. What does Nehemiah's message, "The joy of the LORD is your strength," mean for you today? Now turn the phrases around so that it reads, "Your strength is the joy of the LORD." Does it mean something different to you?
4. God is your Hope. How do you see him revealing hope to you today?

MY PERSONAL JOURNEY

_____

_____

_____

_____

_____

_____

_____

_____

_____

_____

_____

Devotion 24
HOPE AT THE BOTTOM OF THE CYCLE

Be joyful in hope, patient in affliction, faithful in prayer.
Romans 12:12

Your journey through longing for a child is a lot like riding a carousel. On the merry-go-round of hope you ride a mounted steed that rises with anticipation as you start a new cycle, try a new doctor, discover a possible cause, or consider a different option. Then down—your steed slides. Disappointed, your hopes descend. You reach the bottom, but you know you want to hope again. Up you go. You try again. Perhaps you and your spouse agree on a strategy. Maybe you eventually notice that "you're late." Hope buoys you. But down you go again as you experience disappointment. After a few up-and-down cycles—you thought you were getting somewhere—you notice that familiar scenery and sensations signal that you may be back where you started.

This isn't fun anymore. When you hit bottom, you're wiped out.

On morning 28 my basal temperature dropped and so did my hope to conceive a child *again*. My lower back ached, my stomach cramped, and my head throbbed. I knew with certainty that within hours my uterine lining, which I hoped would remain to nourish my child, would pass.

In the face of disappointment, I am strengthened by the life story and writings of the apostle Paul, who understood the true meaning of hope. In 2 Corinthians 11 and 12 he gives a graphic summary of his years of tribulations and persecutions as well as his ecstatic "visions and revelations from the Lord." Talk about an up-and-down ride! He then tells of a "thorn in the flesh" that he asked God to take away. God's response? "My grace is sufficient for you, for my power is made perfect in weakness" (2 Corinthians 12:9). When you're down, God's grace can empower your hopeful ascent as you face another cycle with cautious optimism.

In Romans 5:3–5 Paul gives a definition of hope that may encourage you as you face ups and especially downs in your ride: "We . . . rejoice in our sufferings, because we know that suffering produces perseverance; perseverance, character; and character, hope. And hope does not disappoint us, because God has poured out his love into our hearts by the Holy Spirit, whom he has given us."

Hope is not a positive feeling or outcome. Hope is a lifestyle with an eternal perspective that transcends your desire or disappointment. Hope can be, even if your outcome can't be. Hope is the outcome of suffering, perseverance, and character.

You may be thinking, *This is not the ride I signed up for.* I didn't either. I'd rather get the outcome I want in the way and timing I want. But God sees beyond our temporal ride. Even though we may not understand it, he does have a purpose for our pain. My "down" times of disappointment and loss have changed and refined who I am. My ability to love, show compassion, and demonstrate patience and peace have increased.

I know that God has established all of eternity to make up for what I think I've been deprived of on earth. Now that's a ride I don't want to miss—the never-ending carousel with Jesus and all those who know him personally. Such hope never descends. Desires are fulfilled. Expectations realized. Fullness. Completeness. Life to the full. Around and around and around. Forever and ever. I hope to see you there.

Lord, I feel as if I'm riding the Merry-Go-Round of Hope. My cycle of ups and downs seem to never end. I don't want to experience more disappointment and have to face the same scenery again. Deliver me. Strengthen me. Be my hope. Transform my suffering into perseverance and my perseverance into character . . . and my character into hope.

Give me an eternal perspective. You have all of eternity to fulfill my longing. I look forward to the day I will ride with you, forever and ever and ever. Until then, be my Hope. Amen.

STEPS TOWARD GROWTH

1. Picture yourself on the merry-go-round. Describe the "ups" and "downs" of your ride of hope.
2. When you "hit bottom," what is your response? What does "my power is made perfect in weakness" (2 Corinthians 12:9) say to your situation?
3. Read Romans 5:3–5. Note Paul's definition, involving suffering, perseverance, character, hope. How has your longing to have a child developed your hope?
4. How has God demonstrated himself as your strength and/or your hope?

MY PERSONAL JOURNEY

Father, I love you + desire to serve you. Your
grace is sufficient. I am weak but you are strong.
Father I lay the desires of my heart to have a
child on your altar. Your will be done. I
place my hope in you for eternity. Forgive me
for my weakness. You are the King of Kings.
Father I pray for Kay + Kim — bring a child
to them. Father I pray for Kay's job situation.
Father I pray that you give me opportunity
to share truth to my nieces. Father, thank you for
the healthy child you are bringing into our life.
We will praise you + tell our story, Lord.
We love you Lord.

Devotion 25

HOPE AT 30,000 FEET

The heavens declare the glory of God;
the skies proclaim the work of his hands.

Psalm 19:1

B uckle your seat belts, please, we're ready to take off!" directed the cheery voice.

I clicked my seat belt and grabbed a book from my bag. Sitting on the aisle, I was relieved that no one was sitting next to me, in the middle seat. I rarely get quiet moments to enjoy, so I looked forward to this time to rest and read before I arrived in Missouri for my dad's open heart surgery. Little did I know that God had other plans.

I vowed not to make eye contact with anyone, so I would not be tempted to talk and ruin my quiet time. By the time we reached our cruising altitude of 30,000 feet I had forgotten my vow and introduced myself to the large man sitting next to the window. He looked like an NFL football player. Within a few minutes I discovered he was as an executive for an international security company. His stories fascinated me, but his gentle, humble nature behind his deep, booming voice intrigued me more.

"You sound like a pastor," I said.

"I am . . . part-time," he replied.

Our conversation immediately deepened because we worked for the same CEO, Jesus. Eventually it turned to my work as an author, primarily on the topic of grief.

"Now I know why I got moved to this seat!" he exclaimed. A friend of his had recently lost her baby and a relative had lost her husband. From my bag I grabbed my books, *Grieving the Child I Never Knew* and *Grieving the Loss of a Loved One*, jotted a quick, personal note, and handed them to him.

"Oh, thank you! . . . What's your next book about?"

I gulped: "Infertility."

His laughter surprised me. "Did my wife put you up to this?"

He and his wife longed for a child of their own. I can only imagine what those sitting near us must have thought as they listened to us discuss ovulation, sperm testing, fertility drugs, and timed intercourse. He shared about his fears and his concern about his wife's emotions. I could sense God smiling as I urged him to validate his wife's grief and to do his part to fulfill his portion of the testing.

Three hours passed quickly. When the pilot's voice announced our imminent landing, I stuck the unread book back into my pack. (I never did read that book!) In the airport, the man gave me a hug and thanked me for letting God use me in his life. Though I may never see him again, I look forward to connecting in heaven and seeing what God does in each of our lives.

I am grateful for this divine appointment at 30,000 feet to give hope to another person. I have kept my "unread book" as a tangible reminder to listen and obey God when he asks me to change my plans.

Perhaps God is whispering to you to reach out to another hopeful or hurting person. Don't be surprised if God interrupts your self-absorbed plans, urging you to speak to a stranger or call a friend. God can use your experience to bring hope to others, even if you haven't yet arrived at your hoped-for destination. You may be God's messenger of hope today.

Listen. Obey. Allow Jesus to use your hands and feet and your life experiences to give hope to another person. Your longing for a child and the challenges you have faced may be just the answer someone has prayed for. Go ahead. Reach out.

God, thank you for seeing beyond my circumstances to the people who can benefit from them. Forgive me for becoming so self-absorbed that I fail to see the needs of others. Set my agenda today. Help me to be open to change my schedule if I can be your messenger of hope. Amen.

STEPS TOWARD GROWTH

1. When and how do you close yourself off from others? (Can you think of a few guidelines to help you determine when this is a healthy mechanism and when it is selfish?)
2. If you have become self-absorbed, how have you overlooked the needs of others?
3. How could you be a messenger of hope to your spouse today? To another person?

MY PERSONAL JOURNEY

_____

_____

_____

_____

_____

_____

_____

_____

_____

_____

_____

BRACING

Bracing: *to summon up one's courage; to tighten, clasp, strengthen, or fortify.*

Guard the fortress,
watch the road,
brace yourselves,
marshal all your strength!

Nahum 2:1b

Be on your guard; stand firm in the faith; be courageous; be
strong.

1 Corinthians 16:13 (TNIV)

WHEN HOPE TURNS TO DREAD

[Jesus] got up and rebuked the wind and the raging waters; the storm subsided, and all was calm.

Luke 8:25

I remember one particular month when my temperature ascended to new heights and stayed there, I was excited. "Maybe I'm pregnant!" I told Rich. Although we had flown this familiar course before, this time I allowed my hopes to soar.

Only when I reflected on my previous "false alarm" did I brace myself for another disappointment. Would my temperature descend and cause my emotions and dreams to crash again? I felt as if I were in an airplane, enjoying the ride at 30,000 feet and hearing the pilot warn: "Buckle up. Brace yourself for severe turbulence."

I've often wondered if that's how Abraham felt every month that passed, year after year, without his wife Sarah conceiving a child. Even though God had promised Abraham that he would become the father of many nations, did he always display a hopeful faith? Or were there monthly moments when he recognized Sarah's familiar mood swings and braced himself for another disappointment? And what about Sarah herself? Did she hope for—or dread—the last few days of a cycle?

As for me—clouds of discouragement darkened my hope as I sensed the thunderstorm of dread approaching. Buckled with the truth of God's Word, "I can do all things through Christ who gives me strength," I waited. Although I believed God's truth and trusted God as my pilot, I couldn't imagine facing another disappointment. Only time would tell.

Sometimes God stills the storm, but sometimes he stills *me* long enough to remind me that he is God and will give me courage and calm, no matter what. When my hope turns to dread, I must consciously choose to put my trust in God, the pilot of my life. Although my flight plan may be different than God's, he is the pilot. I must trust him and expect peace.

Your journey through longing for a child may take you to a place where you are soaring in the sky only to hear the thunder-rumble of dread in the distance: "Buckle up! Brace yourself for turbulence!" you think.

Perhaps you look at the calendar and realize your period is due. Maybe you're anticipating—or not—a doctor's report or a call from an agency or a decision from an insurance company. Is the unopened envelope in your hand a thank you note or another baby shower invitation? Are you utterly ambivalent about an upcoming birthday—you always love the celebrations but dread the passing of another year without a child?

When you're in flight, it's normal to brace yourself when a thunderstorm is on the horizon. As dark clouds of doubt loom closer and the wind shears of uncertainty shake your dream, you cling to the seat of your desire and hold on tight. Although you realize you can't control the storm, you can control how you respond to it. Snap. You buckle the belt of truth securely around your waist. Though tempted to scream, you remain silent. You realize that you must trust the pilot to guide you safely through.

Whatever you are bracing for today, be careful to buckle up with God's truth and listen to his voice. He may choose to calm your storm and replace it with a rainbow in your circumstances, or he may calm you with his presence and truth and put a rainbow in your soul.

Lord, I want to soar, but I'm bracing for another disappointment. I feel the dark clouds moving in. Help me buckle up with the truth of your Word and face the next leg of my journey, whatever it may bring. Speak to me. You are my pilot. Guide me safely through this cycle and calm my soul, as I anticipate the outcome of your trustworthy and good will. Amen.

STEPS TOWARD GROWTH

1. What are you facing this week that involves an element of hope and also of dread?
2. How has God calmed your storms in the past? Calmed you?
3. Brace yourself! Buckle up with God's truth! Read Job 38:1; Psalm 107:29; Isaiah 7:4; Luke 8:22–25. How do these Scriptures encourage you?

MY PERSONAL JOURNEY

_____

_____

_____

_____

_____

_____

_____

_____

_____

_____

_____

_____

_____

YOUR SHILOH

[Elkanah] had two wives; one was called Hannah. . . . Year after year this man went up from his town to worship and sacrifice to the LORD Almighty at Shiloh.

1 Samuel 1:2–3

*S*hiloh. Hannah, whose story is found in 1 Samuel 1 and 2, cringed when her husband mentioned the name of the city. She pictured the stone buildings and the crowds gathered outside the tabernacle. She closed her eyes and imagined the symphony of mooing, bleating animals waiting to be sacrificed.

When it was her husband's turn to make an offering, she could picture him walking over to Peninnah and to her children and handing them their portion. She wiped a tear from her cheek as she pictured what it would feel like to face Peninnah again this year and have to listen to children's laughter.

But facing her husband must have been even more difficult. How could she look into his eyes, knowing she had failed to give him a child again this year? *Will I weep continually again this year and ruin our time? Will the priest and others stare at me again and wonder why God continues to close my womb?*

If you remember the story, Hannah's distress was so great that the priest Eli accused her of being drunk. In a later chapter we'll address Hannah's prayer and change of attitude, but here let's look at the reality of her annual trip to Shiloh that provided the setting for her great distress.

You too may have a Shiloh in your life. What place or event do you have to brace yourself to visit or attend? Doctor's office? Family gathering? Baby shower? Mother's Day? Christmas? Baby dedication or baptism? When you hear the word, you may experience a flood of tears because it reminds you of your longing for a child. Perhaps at times you resist going to Shiloh because it is too painful, but eventually you must go. You may feel as if this is the last time you can bear the journey with empty arms. Like Hannah, you may weep and pray, embarrassing yourself and your spouse, confusing your friends or even your pastor.

A few weeks before Mother's Day Linda met with her pastor and shared her personal journey of longing for a child. She urged him to include women who long for a child in his Mother's Day message, prayer, and events. Linda's courage to go to Shiloh resulted in a new Mother's Day strategy in her church and a support group for fertility-challenged women.

Kate wanted to attend her sister's baby shower in spite of her pain. She called a few friends to pray for her. She selected a few Scriptures, wrote them on a note card, and read them daily. She anticipated questions people might ask her and planned her response. She invited her cousin, who was sensitive to her struggle because she had also experienced fertility challenges, to carpool with her and sit with her at the shower. Kate's planning and perseverance paid off, and she enjoyed the event and actually had fun.

Lord, give me strength and courage to face the Shilohs—the places and occasions—that I dread. Show me ways to make these settings seem less threatening to me and even to educate others to the pain of childless couples—with kindness, not judgment. Help me step into my future with confidence and hope, knowing that you are with me in any setting. Amen.

STEPS TOWARD GROWTH

1. Describe places, occasions, or people who represent your personal Shilohs. How can you relate to Hannah at Shiloh?
2. Eli misjudged Hannah. How do you think others have misunderstood you in your journey to have a child?
3. What steps can you take to prepare yourself to face a Shiloh in your life?
4. Read Hannah's prayer in 1 Samuel 2:1–10. How do her words give you hope?

MY PERSONAL JOURNEY

_____
_____
_____
_____
_____
_____
_____
_____
_____
_____
_____
_____
_____
_____
_____
_____
_____
_____
_____
_____
_____
_____
_____
_____
_____

INFERTILITY BALDERDASH

Let the word of Christ dwell in you richly.

Colossians 3:16

Balderdash is a fun word game where obscure words are announced and each team proposes definitions along with the real definition. The team who determines the most correct answers wins. When I've played Balderdash with friends, I usually didn't have a clue what the words meant, but I enjoyed fabricating a definition.

When my infertility doctor suggested a "hysterosalpingogram (HSG)" as one of the routine tests for fertility-challenged couples, I felt as if I was playing Balderdash. Only this time, I wasn't laughing with friends and didn't want to guess at the definition. When the doctor told me about this "painless" medical procedure that would inject dye through my uterus and fallopian tubes, I wanted to reject the definition and search for another. I'd grown suspicious of doctors, especially male doctors who had never experienced the procedure, using words like "painless" or "minimal discomfort." I wanted to pass this seven-syllable word to another player and choose a different word, like conception or pregnant, but I didn't. Instead I braced myself for the procedure.

In the game of Infertility Balderdash I was introduced to a host of new words, many describing procedures I knew nothing about (and didn't want to learn about). To my amazement, my engineer husband, who dislikes spelling and vocabulary, even willingly mastered new verbiage.

Are you feeling overwhelmed with a biological or technological vocabulary that feels beyond your capacity to absorb or comprehend? Are you bracing yourself against the onslaught of technological and biological terms and information—and even insurance terms and forms—that you don't understand? And even more, against the physical discomfort they represent?

Step back. Take one step at a time. Ask questions—of your doctor or the doctor's staff. Ask for clarification. Ask about recommended websites that give reliable information in easy-to-absorb segments. Review the list of resources in the back of this book. Connect with others who may have a personal experience that helps you better define a word you are pondering. (But don't believe every horror story, pain, or trauma you hear, which might only increase your dread unnecessarily. Be discerning when you listen to others. Heed advice from those you know and trust. Wisely weigh personal stories and recommendations.)

As you encounter new words and experiences, remember that your journey is personal. You and your spouse may choose to play or "pass" on any given suggestion or procedure. Even if a doctor persists, there are times when God may lead you to say no.

If you feel that a procedure is ethically acceptable but you are dreading the reality of discomfort or pain (or maybe the financial cost), again, step back. With your spouse and before God, ask what risks you are ready to take to try to have a child.

Ultimately I suggest you turn to the very first word, as described in John 1:1: "In the beginning was the Word, and the Word was with God, and the Word was God." John is describing Jesus. Just a few lines later John says, "In him was life, and that life was the light of men." Let that Word of Life and Light be your strength and guide no matter what new or dreadful words you hear this day.

(And that's no balderdash.)

Lord, I'm overwhelmed with all of the medical jargon and the reality of what the words mean to my experience. Please calm my anxious heart. Give me your wisdom as I discern whether to play or pass. You are my ultimate Word, my Life, and my Light. Reveal your truth and your will. Amen.

STEPS TOWARD GROWTH

1. What new words in your journey have you experienced?
2. What word(s) are you wrestling with? Why?
3. Where could you seek additional information? Consider reviewing the resource section at the back of this book.
4. Read John 1:1–17. List what you learn about Jesus from these verses.
5. What do the words "grace" and "truth" (John 1:17) mean for you as you feel overwhelmed or filled with dread?

MY PERSONAL JOURNEY

_____

_____

_____

_____

_____

_____

_____

_____

_____

_____

_____

_____

_____

_____

Devotion 29
A TALE OF TWO SISTERS

Then came there two women . . . unto the king, and stood before him.

1 Kings 3:16 (KJV)

When one of my friends announced, "I'm pregnant!" I was shocked at my reaction. After I congratulated her, I stomped into my home, slammed the door, and burst into tears. I had been trying to have a child, unsuccessfully, for years, and she had enjoyed one night of unprotected pleasure with her husband—and conceived. Although I had been unaffected by the "I'm pregnant" announcement by countless others, for some reason on that day, I exploded.

Like Jacob's wife Rachel, I wanted what "Leah" had. Remember the story? Though Rachel had Jacob's love, possessions, and a life most women envied, she yearned for what her sister Leah had: children. She despised her sister, who also happened to be Jacob's first wife. (You think you've got a complicated life? Think again!) It seemed as if every time Jacob slept with Leah, Leah got pregnant. Yet Rachel's womb remained empty.

Brace yourself. Sooner or later, like Rachel, you will meet a "Leah," a woman who has what you want. Leahs are everywhere. In your family, your neighborhood, your workplace, and the grocery store. You envy her because she was using contraceptives but still got pregnant or became pregnant the first time she tried. Her Daytimer is filled with OB/GYN and pediatric appointments, while yours charts ovulation and periods.

When I met the "Leah" who reduced me to tears with her "I'm pregnant" announcement, I cried out to God and asked him to help me cope. Amazingly, he connected me to a friend who also longed to have a child. I believe God provided her at a timely season as another "Rachel" with whom I could share my pain and disappointments. Her unconditional love and support helped me to handle my hurts in a healthy, God-honoring way as I encountered more "Leahs" in my journey.

I've discovered that there are Rachels everywhere, although they may be more difficult to spot than Leahs. Trust me, your "Rachel friend" may be your coworker, neighbor, or hairdresser. She understands much of what you are going through and could be a great encourager to you. Look for her. Ask God to connect you to a woman who has "been there, experienced that" and can help you cope with your envy in a God-honoring way. To want what *she* might have— coping skills and comfort—is a good thing.

Until you meet her, I will continue to be your Rachel friend through the pages of this book. Don't forget, God will always be your understanding friend, ready to hold your hand and to connect you to others also.

> *Lord, it seems as if everywhere I look, I see women who have children. I want what they have. I don't know if I can handle one more person telling me, "I'm pregnant!" Help! I feel as if I'm going to explode! Connect me to another "Rachel" who understands my feelings and will provide support in my journey. Amen.*

STEPS TOWARD GROWTH

1. Read the story of Rachel and Leah in Genesis 28–30.
2. How can you relate to Rachel? Who is the "Leah" in your life? How have you responded when others announce, "I'm pregnant!"? Do you brace yourself against the comment?
3. Name a woman who has experienced what you are going through. If you don't know one, ask God to connect you to one, or review the list of organizations in the back of this book and connect with someone.
4. If you have a "Rachel" in your life, take a moment and send her a note to thank her for her support.

MY PERSONAL JOURNEY

Devotion 30

MEN ARE FROM HARDWARE STORES, WOMEN ARE FROM COFFEE SHOPS

It is not good for the man to be alone. I will make a helper suitable for him.

Genesis 2:18

Even after nearly twenty-five years of marriage to the same man, I sometimes look at Rich and wonder where he is from. I expect him to understand how I feel. I want him to listen, but he wants to "fix." You might say he has a hardware-store disposition. He likes to have a list, shop for what he needs, complete the project, and move on. Unfortunately, fertility challenges don't always come with a list of solutions stocked on a shelf. The conversation on the drive to have my second hysterosalpingogram (HSG) went something like this:

"Rich, I hope this HSG is less painful than the first one was! I don't know if I can handle it!" I groaned.

"Maybe you should take a couple of Advil," Rich announced matter-of-factly.

"I did!" I snapped. "It's not fair that I always have to be the one going through all the discomfort."

"Then don't! Let's turn around and go home!" Rich thundered as he screeched the brakes.

"No!" I screamed. "I want to have a baby, but it's obvious that *you* don't or else you would encourage me to have the HSG!"

Looking back through our "communication gaps," I can see that Rich's results-oriented personality had difficulty watching me endure physical and emotional pain. Although he was doing everything on his to-do list to help me, he couldn't take away my hurt. The more I hurt and communicated my disappointments, the more distant I felt he became.

Unlike my hardware store husband, I am more like a coffee shop. The gap between Rich's and my needs and communication styles became apparent when I needed to "venti latte" about everything and anything. I felt hurt when my husband interrupted me, asked me to "get to the point," and gave me a list of solutions. Exasperated after another month of trying I screamed, "Rich, I don't need solutions! I just need you to listen!"

When I verbalized my list of needs to Rich, it's as if the halogen high beams clicked on in his hardware store brain. He felt relieved to know he didn't need to "fix" the problem, rather just give me permission to talk about it, even if the words didn't always seem logical.

If you and your husband are at odds—not necessarily about ethical issues but about more basic communication gaps, misunderstandings that prompt you to brace yourself against each other—read this devotion together and discuss the issue. By God's grand design, men and women are wired differently, to complement each other. With God's help, you can learn to better appreciate those differences.

Lord, I'm hurt again. I don't understand why _____ can't understand my feelings about our circumstances and encourage me. I sense an emotional gap between us. We're living somewhere between the hardware store and coffee shop. We are so different. Forgive us for how we have hurt each other.

You are our Creator and you know everything about us. Help us appreciate our differences and see how you desire us to complement each another. Bridge the gap in our relationship with honesty, love, and forgiveness that come from you. Amen.

STEPS TOWARD GROWTH

1. How are you and your spouse different in your personalities and communication styles? How do you need to hear and receive information? (You and your spouse could answer these questions personally.)

2. Make a list of things you most need from your spouse in regard to fertility issues. (Or it might be a "concerns and questions" list.)

3. Make a date with your spouse this week for conversation about your fertility. Invite Jesus to join you at your outing and to guide your conversation. Bring your respective lists and share with each other your observations, questions, or concerns (see questions 1 and 2). Agree on a specific amount of time to talk. Be gentle with each other. Consider doing this on a regular or as-needed basis. Thank your spouse! (And later treat him to a surprise stroll through the hardware store.)

My Personal Journey

_____

_____

_____

_____

_____

_____

_____

_____

_____

_____

_____

_____

_____

_____

_____

_____

My Personal Journey

GUARDING

Guarding: *a posture of defense or readiness;*
to take precautions; to give protection; keep watch.

Watch and pray so that you will not fall into temptation. The
spirit is willing, but the body is weak.

Matthew 26:41

It was the LORD *our God himself who brought us and our*
fathers up out of Egypt, from that land of slavery, and per-
formed those great signs before our eyes. He protected us on
our entire journey and among all the nations through which
we traveled.

Joshua 24:17

Keep my commands and you will live;
guard my teachings as the apple of your eye.

Proverbs 7:2

Devotion 31
NO TRESPASSING

[Jesus said,] "Here I am! I stand at the door and knock. If anyone hears my voice and opens the door, I will come in and eat with them, and they with me."

Revelation 3:20 (TNIV)

No trespassing!
Keep out!
Beware of dog!
No soliciting!

I thought I could handle going maternity shopping with my niece who was pregnant with her first child, but I was wrong. I actually initiated the outing when we flew back to St. Louis for a family visit. I was happy for her and didn't want my recent miscarriage and fertility challenges to squelch her joy. So I closed the door to my feelings for that afternoon.

Only after we returned home and she modeled her new mother-to-be attire for the rest of the family did I lose it. I excused myself, ran to the bathroom, and locked the door. I slumped to the floor and wept for several minutes, although no one ever knew it. Within thirty minutes I emerged and joined the family with a fresh attitude and a fresh face of make-up.

At times you may feel as if the only way you can survive this journey of longing for a child is to live a guarded life. You may guard your conversations, feelings, hopes, or hurts. Perhaps you even avoid people and gatherings and isolate yourself from relationships for a season. Weary from waiting, wanting, and wondering, you may lock the door to your heart to others. You may hope they sense the signs posted in the yard of your life and walk on by.

Most will. Some may attempt to break through your silence and let you know they care but then retreat when you don't respond. Only a few may understand some of what you are going through and give you permission to stay isolated for a season. In time, they'll return to encourage you, and perhaps you'll be ready to receive what they have to offer.

But only one person understands the reason for your guarded heart. Jesus knows exactly what you are going through and why you are living locked away. He cares. He hurts with you. What you long for matters to him. He will not walk on by.

Listen! Do you hear him knocking at the door to your guarded heart? He is there, waiting to give you hope and comfort in your situation and for all eternity. Walk closer. Press your ear to the door. Feel his presence. Listen to his words, "Here I am! I stand at the door and knock. If anyone hears my voice and opens the door, I will come in."

Now is the time to open the door to your heart to Jesus. Go ahead. Grab the doorknob. Open. And in time, with his help, you'll be able to open your heart again to others.

Lord, I've been guarding myself from others, and at times I've been guarding my heart from you. I'm tired of waiting, wanting, and wondering. I want others to "keep out" and walk on by so I don't have to answer more questions and confront my pain and uncertainty. Forgive me for ways that I have hurt others. Forgive me for avoiding you.

Thank you for your persevering friendship. I know you are there, and I hear you knocking on my guarded heart today. I need you in my life. Right now, I open the door to my heart to you and invite you into my circumstance. Be my strength and courage. Thank you for loving me and for securing my eternal future. You are my Lord and Savior. I know that you are the only way I can get through this. In time, help me to open my heart to others. Amen.

STEPS TOWARD GROWTH

1. In what ways have you been living a guarded life? In your conversation? In your feelings? With your spouse?
2. Who are the people you wish would walk on by? What would you like to say to them?
3. How have you guarded your heart from God?
4. Besides Jesus, with whom do you need to "let down your guard" and invite into your life this week?

MY PERSONAL JOURNEY

_____

_____

_____

_____

_____

_____

_____

_____

_____

_____

_____

_____

_____

_____

Devotion 32

BETTER THAN MASKING TAPE

Out of the same mouth come praise and cursing. My brothers and sisters, this should not be.

James 3:10 (TNIV)

My first grade teacher didn't tolerate excess talking. If students persisted, she simply taped their mouths shut. Brown, gummy masking tape was a regular part of my school attire, though now it would be considered cruel and inappropriate punishment. The worst part was wearing my red marks home after the tape had been ripped off my mouth. Though I still struggle with being quiet and ironically now speak at women's conferences and retreats around the country, I've learned the importance of silence and guarding my mouth, especially when I'm hurt or disappointed with others.

- When my doctor made a cruel remark, I didn't restrain my tongue, but exploded.
- When a well-meaning friend asked how I *really* was handling Mother's Day, I lashed out with unkind words.
- When Rich gave me that knowing look and nodded toward the bedroom, I snapped at him and ruined the intimate opportunity (that time and many others) with my bedroom blues and pessimism.

Oh, how I wish I could erase the audiotape of my words in my journey through longing for a child, but I can't. I know my words hurt others, and I am sorry for that. If only I had heeded my teacher's advice and guarded my mouth.

At times, I felt justified because of the medication I was taking or because I was suffering disappointment that I felt no one understood. But my actions were not justified. In a sense I was in the classroom of learning again, except this time the curriculum was Longing for a Child.

Much like a first-grader I was a novice student; I felt a bit awkward and homesick for things and people that made me feel secure and comfortable. Silence was not my close companion; if I befriended her, I thought I would lose a part of myself and the control I yearned to keep.

Looking back, I regret not wearing masking tape when I went to the doctor, to my bedroom, or to certain gatherings. Though I'm sure most would not have understood my new look, it would have prevented hurtful words from being said that left red marks on the soul of another person.

James 3:3 says that as the bit in a horse's mouth is used to guide it, our tongue has the same kind of powerful influence on us—and others! Words can hurt or help. Speaking words out of emotion or without reflecting on what we say is foolish and harmful. Since God gave us two ears and only one mouth, perhaps he did so to encourage us to listen twice as much as to speak.

Guard your mouth! Be careful what you say to yourself or others. Your words can destroy a mood, a relationship, or an opportunity, or they can enhance it. Even if you feel justified in what you want to say, choose silence and reflection before you speak.

You are a fellow student in the classroom of Longing for a Child. God, your Teacher, is standing in the front of the classroom. He knows you by name and understands why you are frustrated. He knows about the times you've failed to silence your tongue and those you have hurt. Invite him to help you guard your mouth. Learn to listen. Wait. Refrain your words. Embrace silence. And if necessary, buy a roll of masking tape and carry it with you as a reminder to guard your mouth.

Lord, I'm sorry for the words I've spoken that have hurt others. Forgive me. Help me to seek forgiveness from others I've hurt. Silence me. Help me guard my mouth. Empower me to listen and reflect before I speak. Give me self-control. You are my Teacher in the classroom of Longing for a Child. Show me how to use my words to encourage others and give hope. Amen.

Steps toward Growth

1. Reflect on a recent situation when you spoke hurtful words and wished you had worn masking tape.
2. Read James 3:3–6. How does this encourage you?
3. Are you facing a situation or event where you anticipate needing to guard your mouth? Reflect on tangible ways you can do this.
4. Purchase a roll of masking tape this week and keep it with you as a reminder to choose silence or to listen before you speak.

My Personal Journey

_____

_____

_____

_____

_____

_____

_____

_____

_____

_____

_____

GUARDIAN ANGELS

Resist the devil, and he will flee from you. Come near to God and he will come near to you.

James 4:7–8

I love surprises! When my friend Debbie agreed to meet me for coffee and conversation, I wasn't expecting her to present me with a gift. It wasn't my birthday or a special occasion, just an ordinary day.

"Go ahead, open it!" said Debbie as she pushed the colorful gift bag towards me.

I plunged my hand into the tissue paper and pulled out three figurines to add to my angel collection. "When I saw them, I *had* to get them for you!" exclaimed Debbie.

I chuckled at the three ivory-colored cherubs. One stood with its hands covering its eyes. Another sat cross-legged with hands over its ears. The third covered its mouth.

When I got home I placed the three angels on a prominent shelf in my family room. Each day when I see them, I thank God for my friend Debbie. One morning as I strolled past, about to lash out at my husband, those three angel friends caught my attention: "Don't look for trouble! Don't speak!"

But often the message I need to hear is "Don't listen!" I've listened to others' comments and heard what I wanted to hear. I haven't always heard what my friends and family meant to say, but I distorted the meaning and was quick to take offense.

I've also had to close my ears to Satan, who has tried to whisper words of doubt and discouragement. "You're worthless because you can't have a child!" "God is punishing you!" "You wouldn't be a good mother anyway!"

Guarding one's ears is a critical part of guarding one's faith. Sooner or later your faith will be attacked by others. Well-meaning Christians may point their finger at you and command you to "just have more faith." But having faith in faith is distorted thinking. It's not the same as having faith in God regardless of the circumstance. According to Hebrews 11:1, "Faith is being sure of what we hope for and certain of what we do not see."

Faith doesn't guarantee us a problem-free life, but it does promise us the strength to step forward and press on in spite of what is seen or unseen. By faith Noah built the ark. By faith Abraham stepped out and followed God even when he didn't know the destination. By faith Moses led the Israelites into the wilderness even though he didn't have enough food to feed the multitudes. By faith Rahab hid the spies and God saved her family. Your circumstance may be different, but God never changes. He is faithful. He is love. God is . . . even if your child is not. Faith is . . . even if your child is not.

Beware of times when Satan, the liar, tries to tempt you to doubt and distort the truth. He may whisper accusations in your ear and entice you to question God's presence and love. He wants you to turn your back on your faith in God.

Instead of turning your back on your faith, try putting your hands over your ears and tuning out the faithless message. "Get behind me, Satan!" Jesus said. So can you and I.

James 4:7–8 tells us to "resist the devil." The next sentence gives a complementary command: "Come near to God." Ask God to reveal his truth. Then wait. Listen. *Lord, speak to your servant. I'm listening.*

Who knows? Today he may send a friend to give you a guardian angel figurine.

Lord, you are . . . even if my child never is. Nothing can separate me from your love. You are the answer in the midst of my questions. Help me to listen to you and not to my adversary, who wants to distort your truth and destroy my faith. Forgive me for times when I am weak and my faith in you wavers. Strengthen me. Guard my faith with the sword of your Word. Deliver me from the evil one. Amen.

Steps toward Growth

1. "Don't look! Don't listen! Don't speak!" How does this advice encourage you? Describe a time when you have been too quick to listen.
2. What is the difference between faith in faith and faith in God?
3. Read Hebrews 11. What truths do you see here about faith?
4. "Faith is . . . even if your child is not." What does this statement mean to you?

My Personal Journey

Father forgive me for wasting my faith. your plan is good for us. We want to be in the center of your will. Be our source be our light Jesus. We love you Lord Fill the sadness in my heart with your joy —Fill me up with more of you

Devotion 34
GUARDING YOUR BODY

Do you not know that your body is a temple of the Holy Spirit, who is in you, whom you have received from God? You are not your own: you were bought at a price. Therefore honor God with your body.

1 Corinthians 6:19–20

I'm a modest person. During my junior high and high school years I dreaded P.E. because I had to undress and expose myself to others. I never could understand girls who didn't seem to mind baring their bodies in front of others or taking public showers during our class. By contrast, I'd run through the school shower fully dressed just to fulfill the "shower requirement" and wet my hair, which always convinced my teacher. Then I'd hurry to the bathroom stall and change, relieved that I'd successfully guarded my body through another class. I knew God created my body and it was good (a little on the thin side and underdeveloped for most of my younger years—Oh to have that body back now!). However, I believed (and still do) that my body was primarily created for my eyes and my husband's only.

Unfortunately, I had to face the harsh reality that modesty and being fertility challenged are not synonymous. Reluctantly, I trudged to doctor's visits and medical procedures during my fertility-challenged years. I thought it would get easier over time, but it didn't. Each time I was asked to trade in my clothes for a crunchy, backless, paper towel gown, I cringed. Although I may have appeared calm and compliant outwardly, inwardly I felt assaulted and angry. I didn't want to put my body through this. Probing, prodding, and pelvic ultrasounds were a normal part of my infertility P.E. class.

Unfortunately, I couldn't slink away to the stall and hide, though many times I considered it. Too often my doctors, nurses, and technicians lacked the kind of compassion and sensitivity that I desired. Looking back, I wish I had communicated my desires to them instead of ignoring my needs and internalizing my feelings. Only after leaving a doctor's appointment or procedure would I expose my true feelings by screaming or crying in my car.

One day while venting to an empathetic friend about how violated I felt, she wisely asked, "Kathe, how can you guard your body in a loving way?"

This question intrigued me. *Guard my body in a loving way?* I pondered her challenge. I considered ways to protect myself from future emotional and physical assault (or at least minimize it). I painted a picture in my mind of the "ideal setting and staff" and explored proactive steps I could take to make my dream more of a reality.

I also sought God's perspective about my body. When I considered what the Bible says about my body as a believer in Jesus Christ, being a house where God's Spirit lives, I was even more motivated to act. Sometimes it's easier for me to do something for another person than just for myself. I loved God and wanted to please him. I had never considered that I could show love for God by honoring and protecting my body. I asked for his wisdom in how I could guard my body in a loving way, and a multitude of ideas came to mind.

I made a list of my upcoming appointments, procedures, doctors, and technicians whom I would be seeing. If I was unsure about the specifics of a procedure or the person, I sought information. I began to request specific people to whom I felt connected, and most of the time my requests were met. I also talked to other women who had gone through a procedure and got advice. (A great resource today is Hannah's Prayer, a Christian internet support, www.hannah.org.)

In other words, I took charge of my infertility and of my body. With confidence I became my own bodyguard. My mission was to show love to God by showing love in tangible ways to my body. I did everything within my power to make my experience as positive as possible. Here are some of my ideas that may help you guard your body:

- Enlist people to pray for you on the day of an appointment or procedure.
- Invite a friend to go with you (often my husband could not attend).
- Ask for a cotton gown or bring your own (medical supply stores have them).
- Listen to your favorite music on a Walkman.
- Make friends with your technician. (I learned their names, asked questions, brought goodies, sought advice, and asked for special accommodations, such as lights dimmed, cotton gowns, and verbally walking me through the procedure.)
- Treat yourself after your appointment (lunch with a friend, shopping, a manicure, a warm bath, a latte, or a brisk walk in a beautiful setting are possibilities).
- Meditate on a favorite Scripture passage.
- Remind yourself that God loves you, lives in your body if you're a believer in Jesus Christ, and will be with you, no matter what!
- Work out, take a walk, or enjoy a bike ride.
- Take a shower with your clothes on or off . . . it's your preference!

Lord, help! I don't like putting my body through all of this. I feel helpless and out of control. I wish I could skip the tests and procedures. Forgive me for the times I have spoken harsh words to myself and treated my body in an unloving way. Thank you for reminding me that because Jesus is my Lord and Savior, your Holy Spirit lives in me. I am not alone! Teach me to love and protect myself and to take charge of your holy temple. Show me specific steps I can take this week to make my medical process a positive experience and to guard my body. Amen.

STEPS TOWARD GROWTH

1. Reflect on "your body is a temple of the Holy Spirit." How does this make you feel? Does it change your perspective? If so, how?
2. Think about your medical process, the people, that procedure, and the like. What do you need to do to become more proactive and take charge of your body?
3. How can you treat your body in a loving way and "guard your body"? Review the list of suggestions noted above. Circle the ones you would like to try. What other ideas do you have?

MY PERSONAL JOURNEY

_____

_____

_____

_____

_____

_____

_____

_____

_____

_____

_____

_____

YOUR REAR GUARD

But you will not leave in haste or go in flight;
for the LORD will go before you,
the God of Israel will be your rear guard.

Isaiah 52:12

I blame myself for not being able to have children now!" sobbed an unnamed woman at a conference where I was speaking. I listened intently as she recalled her promiscuous past and her three abortions. "I was young," she whimpered. "I didn't know it was wrong then. I'm happily married and desperately want a child, but I can't get pregnant."

Do past regrets ever pursue you and invade your peace about the present and the future?

As the army of past memories marches closer and taunts you with doubt, do you feel disheartened? Although you thought God had delivered you from your Egypt—that is, you've confessed any wrongdoing, you've claimed his salvation, you've accepted his grace—and you've been following him, perhaps you feel deserted in the wilderness. Where is God? Why would he bring you to a barren place like this?

When the Israelites left Egypt and headed toward the Red Sea, Pharaoh's army pursued them. When the Israelites looked up and saw hundreds of chariots approaching them, they were terrified and cried out to Moses, God's representative: "What have you done to us by bringing us out of Egypt? . . . It would have been better for us to serve the Egyptians than to die in the desert!" (Exodus 14:11–12).

Moses answered the people, "Do not be afraid. Stand firm and you will see the deliverance the LORD will bring you today. The Egyptians you see today you will never see again. The LORD will fight for you; you need only to be still." (Exodus 14:13–14)

What happened? "The angel of God" and a representative "pillar of cloud ... stood behind them, coming between the armies of Egypt and Israel. Throughout the night the cloud brought darkness to the one side and light to the other side; so neither went near the other all night long" (Exodus 14:19–20).

Wow. Can you imagine the scene? The Red Sea on one side and Pharaoh's army on the other. Your heart pounds in your chest. Wedged in with no place to run, you wonder what you should do. Then you look up. God himself is between you and the threatening army, protecting you from your pursuing past. He is your rear guard. His cloud sheds light on you, but darkness on Pharaoh's army.

Do you find new courage in this story? God is fighting for you. In your dark night, don't look back; look up! Stay where you are and allow God to fight the fearsome army of regret that pursues you. Cease striving and know that he is your God.

Maybe for one day you need to resist the temptation to fill your time with activity. Give yourself permission to do nothing. Embrace silence. Refuse to think about yesterday—or tomorrow. Choose to ponder where you are now. Today. Look up. See the clouds. Watch them glide across the sky's canvas. Perhaps you see rays of light peeking through them.

Even if you can't see God, he is there. Do you need him to guard you from your past today? He will. Allow him to be your rear guard. He's got your back covered and will fight for you if you let him. Perhaps if you are really still and you listen closely, you'll hear him say to your heart, "Be still! I've got your back covered!"

Lord, be my rear guard today. Fight for me and defeat the fearsome army of regret that pursues me. Forgive me for my past mistakes. Today, I claim your forgiveness. Calm my soul. Help me to look up to you, to cease striving, and to be still today. Amen.

STEPS TOWARD GROWTH

1. What from your past do you feel is pursuing you? If it involves sinful action, read and claim 1 John 1:9 and 3:19–20, verses written to Christian believers.
2. How can you relate to the Israelites and their fear, sensing Pharaoh's army behind them?
3. Read Psalm 46:10. What is keeping you from being still today? How could you guard your schedule from activity so that you can embrace stillness this week?
4. Reflect on God as "your rear guard," standing between you and your past. Each time you look up into the clouds this week, let them remind you to be still; let them remind you that God "has your back covered." He will fight your battles and guard and protect you from your past.

MY PERSONAL JOURNEY

TRUSTING

Trusting: *reliance on the integrity, strength, ability,*
and surety of a person or thing; confident expectation.

He who trusts in himself is a fool,
 but he who walks in wisdom is kept safe.

Proverbs 28:26

Stop trusting in man,
 who has but a breath in his nostrils.
Of what account is he?

Isaiah 2:22

In God I trust; I will not be afraid.
 What can man do to me?

Psalm 56:11

And again,
"I will put my trust in him."
And again he says,
"Here am I, and the children God has given me."

Hebrews 2:13

JOURNEY TO THE WALL

Have I not commanded you? Be strong and courageous. Do not be terrified; do not be discouraged, for the LORD your God will be with you wherever you go.

Joshua 1:9

What outlandish ideas and remedies have others suggested to help you achieve victory in your quest? Sooner or later a stranger or a friend may hand you a list of recommended remedies for your infertility: foods to eat or avoid, shower temperatures, undergarment tips, timing techniques, and postures (like standing on your head). Perhaps your doctor suggests an aggressive strategy to improve your odds of conceiving.

Though outwardly you may nod and smile, inwardly you may scream, *You've got to be crazy!* Maybe you've even felt this way about God as you prayed a specific Scripture and believed you would receive what you asked for. *Am I crazy?* you ask yourself as you stare at the seemingly immovable wall of your childlessness.

I wonder what the Israelites thought when General Joshua, obeying God's command to him, told them to march around the walled fortress of Jericho. Did they question the atypical strategy to defeat this city? How did they feel as enemy soldiers laughed at them while following the priests and the ark of the covenant in a silent stroll, day after day, around the massive stone wall? On the seventh day, when Joshua commanded them to "shout," how amazed they must have been to watch the walls crumble. Victory!

Breaking down your wall of childlessness may require that you do seemingly "crazy" things—which prompts others to laugh in bewilderment and hurl insensitive comments at you. Yet, you continue to march ahead, hopeful that you will achieve victory. Although the massive stones seem immovable, your doctor's strategy seems almost certain to defeat the odds if you are willing to overlook moral choices. As you contemplate what to do, you listen to God's truth and say "no." Though your doctor and the world may label you "crazy," no matter what others think, it is never foolish to obey God.

At times you may have to refuse to follow the advice of others, including your doctor, in order to stay in step with God's truth. Never compromise God's truth and the sanctity of life to try to achieve victory. God's truth may seem crazy to you at times. He may call you to do the opposite of what others suggest: to wait, press on, continue, stop, redirect, consider new options, be silent, or keep marching. His strategies often differ from yours and others. He is your Victor and wants you to be victorious in your quest.

However, his "victory" may look different from yours. Perhaps your wall of infertility will crumble and you will "shout" victoriously, "I'm pregnant!" Or you may sense victory in your spirit and march hopeful into the future, but you still face the physical wall of infertility. You may begin to question if you're crazy because you are coping and calm in spite of the Jericho wall in your life. Trust me, you're not. Peace is God's supernatural gift to you—the ability to press on in spite of your circumstances. Keep marching in step with him. Follow his truth.

Don't focus on the wall, focus on the Wall Crumbler. Even if you march on and don't achieve the victory you have hoped for, don't be discouraged. Perhaps God is crumbling other walls in your life and helping you to live more victoriously. Yes, you may still hurt; you may never understand "why"; you may struggle to be content. That's okay. God knows you're human. He is still your Victor.

Your wall doesn't change who God is. He is still good. He assures us through his Word that he will be the Victor of the final battle. He will defeat the final wall of evil, death, and imperfection. When those of us who know him personally watch the final wall come tumbling down in the final battle between God's kingdom and Satan's, we will shout "Hallelujah" and live eternally in our Victor's presence. Until then . . . keep marching with him, even if it seems crazy to do so. Look for me, I'm marching right beside you.

Lord, I know others don't understand what I'm going through and look at me sometimes as if I'm crazy. I want to follow your truth. Help me march in step with you and make the moral choices you would make, even if my doctor thinks I'm crazy. You are my Victor, and your strategies are often different from mine and those of the world.

Crumble the walls that keep me from knowing you better. Encircle me with your peace and allow me to shout victoriously even if you choose not to remove my wall of infertility. Thank you that I can look forward to living with you eternally. Until then, help me stay in step with you! Amen.

Steps toward Growth

1. Read Joshua 6 for the story of Joshua as he defeats Jericho. What do you think the Israelites thought when they heard the battle plan?

2. Imagine yourself standing at the wall of your circumstances. What crazy situations, advice, or comments have you received from others?

3. Marching in step with God's truth may mean making opposite strategies from what others suggest. What dilemmas are you facing that may require you to follow God's truth instead of human suggestions? What choices have moral consequences?

4. God is your Victor, no matter what! What "other walls" do you sense that God may be crumbling in your life?

5. How can you live victoriously this week, even if your wall of infertility still remains?

MY PERSONAL JOURNEY

_____

_____

_____

_____

_____

_____

_____

_____

_____

_____

_____

_____

_____

_____

_____

_____

_____

_____

_____

_____

_____

_____

_____

_____

_____

IS GOD PUNISHING ME?

For I will forgive their wickedness
and will remember their sins no more.

Hebrews 8:12

I didn't always want to be a mom. In fact, after my parent's divorce, I vowed to myself to *never* have children. I was afraid I would grow up, marry, and divorce too. I certainly did not want other children (especially mine) to suffer the loss of their family through divorce. When my high school friends talked about a future of getting married and starting a family, I cringed. Marriage and motherhood were not my top priorities. Education and pursuing a career motivated me. I often joked and said, "*If* I get married, I'll be at least thirty!"

But God had other plans.

I met Rich when I was a junior at the University of Missouri. Unlike my previous boyfriends, Rich was different. He understood the void I felt from my parents' divorce. His dad died when he was eight and his mom when he was fifteen. Although his loss was different from mine, he empathized with my feelings of fear and uncertainty. To my surprise Rich and I were engaged within nine months. We married shortly after our college graduation.

During the first few years of our marriage, starting a family was not an issue. Then Rich started hinting he'd like to start "trying." But I quickly changed the subject or gave a reason why we should wait longer. The more I resisted, the more he persisted. Finally, I agreed. We assumed I would get pregnant easily, but I didn't. Several months passed. Every twenty-eight days my husband's hopes were dashed when my period started, but I was silently relieved. I felt guilty for not feeling disappointed.

When I realized I was "late" a week before Christmas in 1987, I immediately headed for my doctor's office and took a pregnancy test. A few minutes later the nurse announced, "Kathe, you're pregnant!" I was stunned. I knew I should feel happy, but I didn't, at first. My childhood vow haunted me.

My teenage brother, Doug, was living with us (see Devotion 13, "Prepping for Motherhood"). Rich mentioned to me when I became pregnant that he felt my brother should probably return home. But I couldn't bear the thought of rejecting one child for another. My brother needed love and stability during this time in his life. Would I be able to forgive myself or Rich if we asked my brother to leave and something bad happened to him? In deep anguish, I cried out, "God, please help me!"

Two weeks later, on my husband's thirtieth birthday, I miscarried our first child. I was disappointed, yet I also felt relieved; then I felt ashamed for feeling relieved. I hid my feelings from everyone, including Rich. Only God knew the truth. But would *he* hold it against me?

My desire for motherhood eventually grew, but no child bloomed in my womb. One day after another negative home pregnancy test, I wondered, *Is God punishing me?* Thoughts of my lost child, my previous attitudes about motherhood, and the vow I made as a child flooded my mind. *Is God holding my past against me? Is some hidden sin keeping me from becoming a mom?* It seemed natural to question my Creator and to rationalize possible reasons for my inability to have a child.

Maybe you, too, are searching for answers and wonder if God has a personal payback policy. If so, you can take comfort in the life of Job as found in the book of Job in the Bible (see also Devotion 6, "Who's to Blame?"). His friends and family assumed God was punishing him. But God was not. He allowed Job's suffering, and he allowed mine and yours. God responded to Job in chapters 38–39. Then Job replied to the Lord: "I know that you can do all things; no plan of yours can be thwarted" (Job 42:1–2).

Sometimes there is no answer for suffering. You may never know in this lifetime why you have empty arms. But will you choose to trust God anyway? Do you love God for *who he is* or for *what he does for you?*

Isaiah 55:8 says that God's ways are not our ways. When God doesn't deliver the way you think he should, do you feel unloved or punished? Even if you feel that way, it's not true! God is God. His ways are different from yours. Your suffering may feel like punishment, but it is not. Sure, you may endure natural consequences from your actions, but that doesn't mean God is punishing you. He loves you. He loves you so much he sent Jesus, his only Son, to die for your past and mine. *He* took the punishment, once and for all, for your sin and gave his life to accomplish it. Every sinful thought, action, or attitude of yours is forgiven and forgotten by God because of Jesus.

Perhaps it's time to lay your questions and suffering at the foot of the cross and release them, just as I did. Go ahead, do it now. Like me, you may also need to ask God to forgive you for not trusting him to do things his ways. Embrace God's truth in Hebrews 8:12, that you are forgiven and that your sins are forgotten.

Lord, are you punishing me? Sometimes I feel like it. I'm weary of waiting. Nothing seems to happen the way I think it should. Is some "hidden sin" keeping me from having a child? Your ways are definitely not my ways, but you are still God. You are my Creator, my hope, my comforter, my truth. Forgive me for challenging your sovereignty.

You sent Jesus, your Son, to take my place on the cross and to die for my sins. He took my punishment so I would have hope for an eternal future with you. Today, I lay down my questions and _____ at the foot of the cross. Thank you for your sacrificial, everlasting love. You are not punishing me. I am forgiven. Help me to accept unanswered questions and to trust you, no matter what! Amen.

Steps toward Growth

1. In what way have you felt as if God is punishing you?
2. Reflect on a specific situation recently where God's ways were different from yours.

3. Read Job 38 and 39. Underline the words or phrases that encourage you or give you a fresh perspective of who God is.

4. Even if we disagree with God's plans, God is sovereign. Read Psalm 71:16 and Isaiah 40:10.

5. Personalize Hebrews 8:12 by using your name in the blank: "For I will forgive _____'s wickedness and will remember _____'s sins no more." God is not punishing me! I am forgiven!

MY PERSONAL JOURNEY

Father forgive me for thinking you are punishing me. You are Sovereign King of Kings who loves us so much you gave your son to be our Savior. Thank you Father. Father I have laid down our request to have a child. Open our hearts — give us your wisdom help us to do the path you desire. Help me to face whatever answer you give.

A DOCTOR YOU CAN TRUST

---

*[Jesus] said to her, "Daughter, your faith has healed you. Go
in peace and be freed from your suffering."*

Mark 5:34

H ere are names of Board-certified fertility specialists that may be able to
help you," my doctor announced as he scribbled on a piece of paper.

I stared at the list of unfamiliar names. I had hoped this day would never
arrive. I trusted the doctor sitting across the desk from me. We shared an open,
honest, long-term relationship. I had hoped he would be able to help us achieve
success, but I had to face reality.

At that moment, I felt as if I was standing at a relational fork in the road.
Which way should I go? Whom should I trust to take me farther in my journey? I hugged my doctor good-bye. Although I felt uncertain about my next
steps, I knew I needed to leave the familiar and be willing to trust again—
someone else.

Sooner or later, you too may reach a fork in the road and have to make the
decision to step out in a new direction with new medical companions. Starting
over and building a new relationship with a doctor can feel overwhelming.

Be patient. Shop around. Find out as much as you can about the potential
doctor's credentials and personality. Talk to other patients. Ask for an information interview. Ask questions such as these:

- Will the doctor be involved in all of your procedures, or will the
  support staff do some of the treatment plan?

- Is the doctor known for suggesting procedures to fit a patient's needs, or does the doctor prefer a certain strategy?
- Is the doctor sensitive to how your faith influences your decision-making?
- Is the doctor's office equipped to administer tests?
- If not, where will you need to go?
- How flexible is the doctor with insurance, payment plans, and so on?

Connecting with a doctor and building a level of confidence and trust may take time. Rich and I had positive relationships with two fertility doctors; after our first meeting we felt comfortable pursing a relationship. However, a third doctor, who came highly recommended from friends, enraged me so much with his insensitivity and selective approach that eventually I terminated the relationship.

Letting down your guard to trust your doctor is essential for you and your spouse. You may have to see several before you sense the right fit. Don't give up. Persevere until you find a doctor you can trust.

That's what an unnamed woman in the Bible did. Mark 5:24–34 says she suffered gynecologically under the care of doctors for twelve years. While her friends were playing with their children and decorating their homes, she was at the doctor's office or trying to find one. Yet she persevered and dared to trust once more—Jesus, a Healer, the Great Physician. When he came to town, she dared to reach out and touch his robe, in faith, with trust. She connected with him as with no other doctor she had ever met. Immediately she was healed.

Are you facing a fork in the road? Do you need to leave the land of familiar and forge ahead into the land of uncertainty? Whom will you need to trust to help you journey on? A new doctor? Your spouse? A counselor? Your pastor? A friend? God?

Like the unnamed women who dared to persevere and trust again and again, you can too. Gaze into the eyes of Jesus, your Great Physician. Trust him with your uncertainty, your future, and your fears. Touch his robe. Does he have the power to heal you? Absolutely.

But even if Jesus doesn't heal you in the way you desire, he is still trustworthy. He may bring healing to you in other ways. Talk to him about your situation. Invite him to walk with you in your journey. Ask him to help you have faith to trust again. Your Great Physician is waiting to connect with you today.

Lord, I'm at a fork in the road in my journey. I don't know which way to go and whom to trust. Give me faith to persevere. Help me to trust again. Lead me to those I can relate to and will help me journey beyond where I am today. Heal me, Lord. You are my Great Physician and able to do all things. Heal my broken dreams, anxious heart, relationships, body, mind, and spirit. Touch me with your truth and enable me to trust your plan. Amen.

STEPS TOWARD GROWTH

1. Read the story in Mark 5:24–34. How does this story encourage you to trust?
2. What fork in the road are you facing?
3. Whom do you need to trust?
4. Make a list of questions you would like to ask this person to build your relationship and clarify any concerns you have.

MY PERSONAL JOURNEY

_____

_____

_____

_____

_____

MY PERSONAL JOURNEY

_____

_____

_____

_____

_____

_____

_____

_____

_____

_____

_____

_____

_____

_____

_____

_____

_____

_____

_____

_____

_____

_____

_____

Devotion 39
WHAT'S IN THE BROWN BAG?

There is a time for everything
and a season for every activity under heaven . . .
a time to weep and a time to laugh.

Ecclesiastes 3:1, 4a

D
o you want to trade what you have for door number one, door number two, or the big bag on the showroom floor? I can still remember watching the popular game show *Let's Make a Deal* as contestants anguished over their decision to win a prize. Sometimes they lucked out and won a car or some other elaborate gift, but often bells clanged and the crowd laughed when their "prize" turned out to be a goat. I wondered what the contestants did with the goat and how they really felt about being publicly humiliated.

My husband, Rich, can relate. In the 1980s when our doctor handed him a brown bag to obtain a sperm count, I can still recall his analytical, engineer look and his bewildered response: "You want me to do *what?*"

As if to say, "Let's make a deal," Rich listened to the options of tests available and reluctantly chose the brown bag, though I know he would have traded this option for a goat (or for a new method they have recently developed through a sperm collection condom that can be used through natural lovemaking). He had to trust and believe that this was a necessary step. Oh the things men do for love and to become a dad.

"What's in the brown bag?" became our private joke as it sat empty on our kitchen counter day after day. I didn't want to nag or pressure him about it, but one day the Type-A driven part of my personality kicked in and I finally blurted, "Do you want *me* to deliver the goods to the lab?"

"Would you?" he said with sigh of relief. Although we'd been married for nearly a decade and I thought I knew my husband, at that moment I looked at this six-foot-two man and realized I had never stopped to consider *his* feelings about our quest to have a child. I just assumed that he, like me, would be a good contestant. Poking, prodding, and physical humiliation had become part of my weekly routine. But for Rich, this was a new adventure. (At that time we were less mature in our faith and were unaware of Christian views on masturbation, although we believed [and still do] that using pornography is sin.) And at that time there was not yet available the recent medical option for obtaining a sperm sample by using a special condom design for this purpose.

The next day I walked into the lab's waiting room, bag in hand, and plopped it on the counter. The nurse gave me that knowing look and smiled. *That wasn't so bad*, I thought as I turned to leave. But before I could exit, a different nurse yelled, "Wait! Whose brown bag is this?" I looked around the waiting room at chairs full of others holding brown bags. *Oh dear*, I thought, *I had cut in line*. At that moment I considered walking out the door and ignoring her, but I didn't. I sashayed back, grabbed my bag, and said, "It's *my husband's*, thank you very much!"

At dinner that evening I recalled the day's happenings, and we celebrated another milestone in our journey. "What's in the brown bag?" is a phrase that still can bring a chuckle.

Is it time to give yourself permission to lighten up and laugh? Although you may feel that every private area of your life is publicly exposed, know that others before you have experienced the humiliation. Also remember that this is a season that won't last forever. Sooner or later all game shows come to an end, and so do the tests and procedures. In the meantime, ask God to give you the gift of laughter and creativity. Even if you get a goat or two along the way, you'll make it through.

God, increase our sensitivity for each other and show us how to communicate with care. Help us to lighten up and find humor, even in our humiliation. Help us laugh. Be our guide through the every season of our journey. Amen.

STEPS TOWARD GROWTH

1. How are you and your spouse responding differently to your situation?

2. It's been said that the difference between laughter and tears is sometimes a matter of one's perspective. Try to think of one experience you've had that may have seemed humiliating, but could be viewed with humor. (If you can't think of one, ask God to show you.)

3. God created laughter. Read Genesis 21:6; Psalm 126:2; Proverbs 31:25; Ecclesiastes 3:1, 4; Luke 6:21. Write these verses on a 3 x 5 card and refer to them when you need a reminder to laugh.

4. Anticipate—and carry out this week—one way to encourage your spouse to laugh.

MY PERSONAL JOURNEY

_____

_____

_____

_____

_____

_____

_____

_____

_____

_____

WINTERTIME TRUST

I tell you the truth, unless a kernel of wheat falls to the ground and dies, it remains only a single seed. But if it dies, it produces many seeds.

John 12:24

I t's winter. The birds are silent. The nights are long. Barren branches stand alone in the dark wondering if the Creator has forgotten his creation. *Where are you, God? Have you abandoned us? Why do you ignore our pleas for fruitfulness? Why do you feel so far away? Don't you care? Why won't you rescue us from the pain of freezing cold? Will we ever feel the warmth of your presence again? Will the sun ever shine in our soul again?*

In your journey perhaps you have experienced winter—a season of feeling stripped down and naked. You cry out to God but only sense his silence and rejection. You plummet to the depth of aloneness. Some refer to this as "a dark night of the soul" or "wilderness times." I think of these times as seasons of spiritual barrenness. Your relationship with God seems dark, distant, and disconnected. Your prayers seem to hit a spiritual ceiling and bounce back. God seems unreachable, and his voice is quiet.

Though outwardly you seem unproductive spiritually or disconnected from God, it is during this season of winter when you must embrace rest and allow the Gardener to prune you. Pruning is painful. As God snips away unhealthy relationships, wrong attitudes, hidden resentment, unforgiveness, anger, and unrealistic expectations, you may not feel "loved" by him. Doubt and self-pity may try to become your friend, but resist them. God is there even if you don't see his productive hand at work. He is there even in the silence. Trust him through your season of winter.

During this time of rest, the sap in your life is going deep into the life roots. Don't rely on outward signs and feelings. God is doing an inner work in your life. Though you don't see the evidence of fruit, it is in process. Your character and trust is being shaped. Inward fruit. Will you trust your Creator even if you don't hear his voice as you did in earlier days? Are you willing to surrender your feelings and expectations to him in spite of what you think they should be?

During this winter season, God wants to redirect you to know him in a deeper way. Your season of spiritual barrenness is really not barrenness at all, but a time to reflect, regroup, and root yourself in God. He is trusting *you* with his silence and waiting to see how you will respond. Continue to talk to him. Listen. Wait. New life is budding beneath the snow of your soul, even if you don't see it. But God does. In his perfect timing, winter will pass. Spring will come. The sun will rise in your soul again.

But until then, stay connected to God. Stay rooted in his Word. Don't allow the darkness of your situation to discourage you. Don't allow his silence to deceive you. He loves you and will never leave you. Every tear, prayer, and question is important to him. His desire is that you will live connected to him and bear "much fruit."

I am praying that for you right now. I am also praying that God will open your womb to become fruitful or to fulfill your desire for a child in a spiritually miraculous way. Apart from him you can do nothing. I am smiling as I picture clusters of ripe fruit among leafy green branches filled with chirping birds on the trunk of your tree. And I sense God smiling too through the sunshine.

Lord, are you there? Do you hear me? I feel so alone. The darkness is closing in. Have you abandoned me? No. Your Word says you will never leave me, no matter what. You love me and even if I don't feel it, I believe you. Help me stay rooted in the depths of your Word. Prune me from people, things, and attitudes that will stunt my growth. Nourish me so that spring growth with burst forth from my spirit.

Deepen my relationship with you, Lord. I want to bear much fruit for you. I know that apart from you I can do nothing. Help me stay connected, no matter what. And open my womb to become fruitful or fulfill my desire for a child in your miraculous way. Amen.

Steps toward Growth

1. Describe your relationship with God during a winter season.
2. Hannah, Abraham, Job, Paul, and even Jesus experienced times when they didn't sense God's presence. When Jesus cried out, "My God, my God, why have you forsaken me," he expressed his feelings of abandonment. Yet, in time, God produced "much fruit" from Jesus' suffering and "the dark night of his soul." How do these models or others encourage you?
3. How do you sense that God is pruning or reshaping you today?
4. Read and reflect on John 15:5–12. What does it mean for you to "remain" in him?

My Personal Journey

_____

_____

_____

_____

_____

_____

_____

_____

Section Nine

RELEASING

Releasing: *to free from confinement,*
bondage, obligation, pain; let go; surrender.

O LORD, *truly I am your servant;*
I am your servant, the son of your maidservant;
you have freed me from my chains.

Psalm 116:16

He has sent me to bind up the brokenhearted,
to proclaim freedom for the captives
and release from darkness for the prisoners,
to proclaim the year of the LORD's *favor*
and the day of vengeance of our God,
to comfort all who mourn,
and provide for those who grieve in Zion—
to bestow on them a crown of beauty
instead of ashes,
the oil of gladness
instead of mourning,
and a garment of praise
instead of a spirit of despair.

Isaiah 61:1b–3a

LET'S GET REAL

He searches the sources of the rivers
and brings hidden things to light.

Job 28:11

I could hardly wait to get to the retreat in 1992 and enjoy pine trees, laughter, campfires, and uninterrupted time with God. I needed a break from Rich and my toddler son Jake (whom we adopted in 1989). My friend Lisa and I had planned every detail of the women's weekend. Our theme? "Let's Get Real." I knew the participants had hidden hurts. Little did I know that God wanted to use the program to touch me.

Our final session arrived much too quickly. We sang "Open the Eyes of My Heart, Lord," and then left the chapel to be alone with God for a while. Lisa handed each woman a helium balloon and a black marker. "Ask God to show you an area of your life you need to release to him and write it on the balloon," she instructed. I considered skipping this exercise to start on clean up, but I didn't want to miss a final opportunity to enjoy the brisk breeze and trees before I returned home to the blazing, barren desert.

I plopped down on a stump in a pine grove. I closed my eyes and listened. I opened my eyes and stared at my balloon. As I mentally sorted through my checklist of relationships, I felt as clean as the balloon. *God open the eyes of my heart . . . is there anything there I need to release to you?* I waited—and waited.

Finally my thoughts drifted to a time a year earlier when I pursued more medical treatments to try to conceive a sibling for our son. *Where did that thought come from?* I wondered. I was happy being the mom of an only child and had already accepted the reality that I would have no more children even though doctors could not explain the specifics of why I could not conceive. *What are you saying to me God?* I waited. I popped off the lid to the marker and wrote: CONTROL. Relieved to have written something, I stood up to head back, but my mind flooded with more words. *Was this God or my overachiever nature kicking in?* I wasn't sure, but the faster I wrote, the better I felt.

Then the doctor's office nagged again. *Let's get real, God. What are you trying to tell me?* In large bold letters I wrote: INFERTILITY. I slumped to the ground in tears. It had never occurred to me to release my infertility. In fact, I thought I already had, because I had an adopted son and was moving on with my life. I knew that God was in control and thought I had accepted his plan for me as a mother. Yet as I gazed at the word, I knew that God was right. I had never "formally" released my infertility to him.

Moments later I stood in a circle with other women holding helium balloons, which we released to God. As I watched my balloon soar, I could almost picture God catching my balloon and smiling. Although I still didn't know what the future held for my life concerning more children, for the first time I could rest in the confidence that I had released my infertility to God. This was a spiritual marker, a life-changing moment God would continue to use to strengthen me through seasons of discouragement and doubt.

Consider today as an opportunity to allow God to open the eyes of your heart. Have you ever "formally" released your infertility to God? You may want to find, or imagine, a balloon. Ask God to reveal anything you need to release to him. Listen. Wait. With a marker, write down what comes to mind. Now release it. Remember this moment as you watch your balloon float skyward into the hands of God. You may want to record today's date and what you released in a special place, so when these issues resurface in the future, you can remind yourself, *I already released that!*

> *Lord, let's get real. Open the eyes of my heart. Be my truth. Create in me a pure heart and renew a right spirit within me. Search my heart and reveal to me what you see hidden there. What do I need to surrender to you? Today I release _____ to you. (date) _____. Amen.*

STEPS TOWARD GROWTH

1. Let's get real: What do you need to release to God?
2. Is there an area of your life you thought you had released but you seem to keep struggling with? What is it?
3. Read Job 28:11 aloud as your personal prayer to God. On this page or on an environmentally safe helium balloon, write down any thoughts that come to mind. Write down today's date. Now release it to God.

MY PERSONAL JOURNEY

_____

_____

_____

_____

_____

_____

_____

_____

_____

_____

_____

_____

_____

_____

Devotion 42

THE MOUNTAIN OF SURRENDER

So Abraham called that place The LORD Will Provide.
Genesis 22:14

The story of Abraham in Genesis 22 about his willingly laying his son Isaac on the altar of sacrifice is one of the most dramatic in the Bible. An important lesson here is that if we are willing to give to God what we treasure the most, he will provide. Maybe not a dramatic miracle, but strength and peace and blessing—whatever he knows we need for the moment.

One day when I was thirty-seven, after adopting our son and after years of waiting to conceive again, I clutched a positive pregnancy test. But a few weeks later I discovered the child I carried had a fatal birth defect. I began a bittersweet journey up the mountain of surrender. Though doctors gave me the option of aborting, I knew God had a purpose for my child's life. Most people, even some Christians, didn't understand why I would obey God's call to carry my son to term. Yet I sensed that God was leading me by the hand, whispering, "Surrender your thinking. Don't listen to others. Follow me even if it doesn't make sense."

Throughout my journey I learned a lifetime of lessons. I learned that living a surrendered life is more than a one-time commitment; it is a process that requires moment-by-moment release. For me this meant surrendering my plans for my child's future and releasing my expectations of what I had hoped motherhood would be like.

I still don't fully understand why God allowed me, a barren woman, to conceive a child destined to die. Perhaps he knew that my years of longing had changed me. I was ready and willing to trade my empty womb for a child, even if it meant I would not get to know my child fully. All I know is God called me to carry my son up the mountain and surrender my outcome to him. Month by month, I climbed higher in my faith. I knew God was able to perform a physical miracle and trusted that he would. "But even if God doesn't," I testified, "I will worship him." About the time I thought I was "surrendered up," I discovered I had more to release to God: my feelings, my pride, my fears, my anger, my resentment, my questions.

Finally, it was time to surrender my child to birth. I felt God's presence and power, yet I was reluctant to journey those few final steps to my altar of labor and delivery. My son's life depended on me. When they cut the umbilical cord, he could not survive and live on earth—without God's dramatic intervention. Only with and by God's strength could I let my son go, from my womb. As I held him in my arms, I was overwhelmed with God's peace. As I released John Samuel's earthly life to his eternal life in heaven, I sensed God smiling. Without God's power and presence in my life, I never could have made this sacrifice and surrendered my son. I continue to grieve his loss, but God continues to provide himself daily as my comforting teacher and companion to help me surrender my pain, my unfulfilled longing, my heart, and my future to him. This experience of having a son, who was born only to die, enabled me to draw closer to the feelings of God, who sent his Son who was born to die.

Perhaps now is the time to carry whatever God is asking you to release up the mountain. Go ahead. Walk closer. Lay it down on the altar. Let go. Now walk away. Leave it there. The Lord Will Provide (Jehovah Jireh) is one of the Hebrew names for God. It is what Abraham called his mountain of sacrifice. God will provide what you need. Allow him to provide you with peace. He will give you the strength and courage you need. Trust him in this moment and in future moments when you sense his calling you to lay something else down.

Lord, I want to live a surrendered life. Give me courage to obey you and climb up the mountain to surrender _____. I know you are able to do all things, and I believe you are a God of miracles. I know you can fulfill my longing, but even if you choose not to fulfill it in the way I hope for, I will worship you. You are Jehovah Jireh, the God who provides. Give me your courage to obey you willingly and trust you completely in all things. Today, this moment, I release _____ to you. Give me your strength to walk away and not pick it up today. Amen.

STEPS TOWARD GROWTH

1. Read the story of Abraham and Isaac in Genesis 22.
2. How does this story encourage you to live a surrendered life?
3. How has God demonstrated himself to you as Jehovah Jireh (The LORD Will Provide)?
4. What is God asking you to surrender today? What is keeping you from releasing it?
5. Pray the above prayer, asking God to strengthen your faith today.

MY PERSONAL JOURNEY

_____
_____
_____
_____
_____
_____
_____
_____
_____
_____
_____

Devotion 43

ATTITUDE CHANGE

*[Hannah said,] "I have been praying here out of my great
anguish and grief."
Eli answered, "Go in peace."*

1 Samuel 1:16–17

The biblical account of Hannah in 1 Samuel 1–2 starts by laying out the
family dynamics. A man named Elkanah had two wives. Peninnah had
many children. Though Hannah had her husband's undying love, she was barren. Once a year the family traveled to Shiloh to worship God.

Elkanah had hoped that this year Hannah would have conceived. But no.
He could tell by her red-streaked face that Peninnah, flaunting her sons and
daughters, had provoked Hannah to tears *again. I feel so helpless and want to
take away Hannah's sorrow. What else can I do?* "Hannah, why are you weeping?
Why don't you eat? Why are you downhearted? Don't I mean more to you than
ten sons?" (1 Samuel 1:8).

I can only imagine Hannah's anguish at hearing these words. He had
fathered a child. How could he relate to the rejection and emptiness she felt?
Her longing for a child could not be compared to her husband's love. Although
he lavished her with affection and gifts, he could not take away her pain. Her
husband provider could not fix this problem. Knowing this, she turned to her
heavenly Father and poured out her grief and her desire with so much emotion
that bystanders thought she was drunk. She vowed to God that if he would give
her a son, she would give him back to the Lord. Having laid her burden before
God, she was able to "go in peace."

Scripture says that she was no longer downcast. Did she radiate an inexplicable confidence and peace? In the following weeks, perhaps she initiated conversation with her husband on topics other than children. Was her new attitude reflected in the bedroom? Did she respond to her husband's touch in a new way—with a heart to please him and a fresh freedom to enjoy their intimate moments rather than its being a purpose-driven time of baby-making?

In time, Hannah did conceive and gave birth to Samuel. Does that mean if you pour out your heart to God, you too will conceive and have a child? I don't know what plans God has for you. I do know that he is aware of and present in your tears and anguish. When you feel alone in your quest and wish your spouse could understand exactly what you are going through, God hasn't rejected you or your request. He is there. Perhaps the Lord is saying, "Why are you downhearted?" Pour out your grieving heart to him. Go ahead. Tell God exactly how you feel. He is waiting to hear. He wants you to release your burden to him today.

God's desire is that you, like Hannah, would "go in peace." Anticipate a change in your attitude. See if others notice too. Perhaps you will sense a fresh breeze blowing through your soul and you'll be able to make it through the day or week without tears, anger, frustration, or resentment. Open to new topics of conversation with your spouse, and you may discover a new level of intimacy in your romantic encounters. Who knows what changes your new attitude will bring?

Lord, can we talk? I feel so helpless in my journey. I can't seem to fix the problem and achieve the results I yearn for. Today I pour out my heart to you about_____.

Give me your peace. Change my attitude. Fill my soul with a fresh breeze. Help me to hope and help in new ways. Enlarge my mind, heart, and conversation. Enable me to love my spouse the way my spouse needs to be loved today. Amen.

STEPS TOWARD GROWTH

1. Read 1 Samuel 1:1–20 from Elkanah's prospective. Identify his frustrations. Then read it from Hannah's perspective. How are her frustrations different?
2. How does this story encourage you?
3. Take your hurts, desires, disappointments, and pain to God. Don't be afraid if an emotional dam breaks. Eventually get up, wash your face, and fix yourself a snack.
4. Invite God's peace to infiltrate your heart. How can you demonstrate God's peace in your life and respond differently to your spouse or others this week?

MY PERSONAL JOURNEY

_____

_____

_____

_____

_____

_____

_____

_____

_____

_____

_____

_____

WHO'S CALLING?

"The LORD was not in the earthquake. . . . The LORD was
not in the fire. And after the fire came a gentle whisper. When
Elijah heard it, he pulled his cloak over his face and stood in
the mouth of the cave.
Then a voice said to him, "What are you doing here, Elijah?"
1 Kings 19:11–13

At some point in this journey of longing for a child, it's good to stop and ask some basic questions about your calling to and expectations for motherhood.

I remember a conversation I had with a woman named Dee, who was getting a lot of pressure from her friends and family that she *should* have children. She and her husband loved to teach youngsters at church and were constantly being told, "You'd be such great parents." Dee and her husband were content to live child-free, enjoy their careers, travel, and give their time, talent, and treasure to help others. However, one day when a Christian friend made a flip remark that she was being selfish and not fulfilling God's purpose for her life, she blew!

I also think of my friend Jan, who didn't want a child until she was in a second marriage and well into her thirties. Being close with her own mother, Jan realized she wanted a daughter so she could one day have a similarly close mother-daughter bond.

For reasons unique to their own situations, ultimately neither Dee nor Jan actively continued the pursuit to have a child. And their journeys prompt me to raise questions for you to consider as you look at your own desire for a child:

- Is having a child more important to you than to the people around you?
- Try to imagine your current situation but without any pressure you feel from family or friends. Would your longing be as strong?
- Is your longing for a child a result of a longing that God has implanted in your heart or a longing your mother has laid on you? (The two aren't necessarily mutually exclusive, but they might be.)
- Fast forward your life and try to imagine yourself as a mother of a colicky baby, of a demanding two-year-old, of a fidgety seven-year-old, of a tear-your-hair-out teenager. Think of yourself in old age. Do you see yourself with or without children?
- What if your grown children were to disappoint you, or predecease you? (If you want children "only" to guarantee your caretaking in old age, think again.)

Any of these questions—and others—can help you determine when it might be time to "push stop" and release the burden of your desire, if indeed it feels like a burden.

In the Old Testament book of 1 Kings, the prophet Elijah is worn out, depressed, and hiding in a cave, when God makes it clear that he wants to speak to him. Elijah waits. A tornado tears at the mountain. But "the LORD was not in the wind." Then an earthquake came, but that wasn't the Lord's voice either. Then a fire. But neither was that God speaking. But after all the moving and shaking, Elijah heard God's voice as a "gentle whisper," which resonated a question: "What are you doing here?" He asked Elijah to reconsider his situation, to "go back," and yet ultimately to go forward and anoint Elisha.

Maybe God today is simply asking "What are you doing here?" not in a loud voice but with a whisper. Who is calling you to motherhood? And what does motherhood mean for you?

God, what am I doing here? What does motherhood mean to me? I've been listening to the clamor of other voices urging me to have a child. I don't want to please others but only you, God. Give me discernment. Close my ears to the noise and remove the pressure I feel. Reveal your desire for my life. Is my longing for a child from you? Are you calling me to motherhood? Whisper your truth to my heart today. Amen.

STEPS TOWARD GROWTH

1. Who is calling you to motherhood? In what settings (with family, friends, church) do you feel pressured to become a mother? How have you responded?
2. What are you doing here today? What does motherhood mean to *you*?
3. Is your longing for a child from God or others?
4. Close your ears to others' voices. Listen for God's whisper. What is he saying to you today?

MY PERSONAL JOURNEY

_____

_____

_____

_____

_____

_____

_____

_____

_____

_____

Devotion 45

SEASONS OF SURRENDER

You can't heal a wound by saying it's not there!
Jeremiah 6:14 (TLB)

Jeff walked by the Christmas tree and the mantle where three stockings hung. To his surprise an overwhelming wave of sadness crashed his soul. Memories flooded his mind of past celebrations with his wife, Cindy, and their son, Matt. Family traditions. Laughter. Lots of food. Piles of presents—bicycles, baseball mitts, electric guitars. Jeff gazed at his son's picture on the wall. *Is Matt really a senior already?*

Although Jeff had experienced numerous graduations of kids from his youth group, he never considered what it would feel like to be the *dad* saying good-bye. But this Christmas represented an ending to a season he thought would never end. Even though he and Matt shared a great relationship and would continue to connect, the thought of Matt's moving out made him feel uncomfortable. He and Cindy, empty-nesters? Impossible. *I miss Matt already and he isn't even gone.* Jeff yearned to slow down the rapid pace of life.

Jeff experienced another surprise. He didn't expect that this season of change would trigger the pain of another loss years earlier, when he nearly lost Cindy through an ectopic pregnancy. *Our child would be 14,* Jeff thought. *What would life be like with another child at home? Wasn't this empty-nest season arriving prematurely?*

Jeff rewound the tape of their journey to have more children. The miscarriages. Failed adoptions. Operations. He fast forwarded through the times of waiting, disappointment, anger, and questioning until he reached the end of the tape—surrender and acceptance. Although he and Cindy had agreed to push "stop" years earlier and felt they had done everything possible to have another child at that time, he wondered if God was directing them to push "play" again. Should they consider becoming foster parents or adopting an older child? Or perhaps God was directing Jeff to grieve and to embrace his pain. Could this be the new season of surrender?

Like Jeff, you may discover that a change or a holiday triggers feelings about the child you lost or long for. Perhaps you are surprised at the deep emotional pain that surfaces. The empty place in your heart is exposed again. Even though you may try to fill it with answers, work, your spouse, your ministry, or God himself, you may still feel the void. Give yourself permission to grieve. Weep if you need to. Reflect. Talk to God. Share your feelings with your spouse. Release your anger or questions. Seek professional help from a Christian counselor or your pastor.

Letting go is a process that may take a lifetime and may cycle seasonally, as you release new (or rerelease old) questions, emotions, disappointments, expectations, fear, anger, or "empty slices" in your heart or home. Although you may never fully understand the why of your situation until eternity, you can always pour out your heart to the One who understands. He loves you and will walk with you through the empty rooms of your heart or home and will lead you to others who may provide the comfort you need.

Lord, I'm hurting. I don't understand my feelings. Why am I hurting after all of this time? Rewind the memories of my past and show me the truth. Show me the purpose in my pain. Invade the empty space in my heart. Comfort me. Do you want me to push "play" again and pursue new options to have a child, or are you bringing me to a new place of acceptance? Guide me through this season of surrender. Help me journey through the questions, options, emotions, anger, and pain so that I can reach a place of acceptance. Connect me to people who will support me in this season. Amen.

STEPS TOWARD GROWTH

1. What occasions (such as graduations) or seasons (such as Christmas) have triggered your longing for a child?
2. What future seasons or events do you anticipate being difficult for you? How can you help prepare yourself to encounter new grief?
3. What does Jeremiah 6:14 (TLB) say to you today: "You can't heal a wound by saying it's not there"?
4. Read Ecclesiastes 3:1–8. Allow God to speak his seasonal word to you—about acceptance or surrender—through this Scripture.

MY PERSONAL JOURNEY

_____

_____

_____

_____

_____

_____

_____

_____

_____

_____

_____

_____

_____

_____

_____

_____

MY PERSONAL JOURNEY

Father my heart is saddened - but you
already know that. You know the desire of our hearts
Forgive me for not being patient. Father
I love you - open my eyes to the people around me
today so we can show your love. Open doors
we need to walk through + close doors
that are not the path for us.
Fill the desires of my heart to be
a mother - I surrender this
dream to you - fill it in your time

REDIRECTING

Redirecting: *to change the direction or focus of.*

Direct my footsteps according to your word;
    let no sin rule over me.

Psalm 119:133

I am the LORD your God,
    who teaches you what is best for you,
    who directs you in the way you should go.
If only you had paid attention to my commands,
    your peace would have been like a river,
    your righteousness like the waves of the sea.

Isaiah 48:17b–18

I waited patiently for the LORD;
    he turned to me and heard my cry.
He lifted me out of the slimy pit,
    out of the mud and mire;
he set my feet on a rock
    and gave me a firm place to stand.
He put a new song in my mouth,
    a hymn of praise to our God.

Psalm 40:1–3a

OBSTRUCTION OR OPPORTUNITY?

"For my thoughts are not your thoughts,
neither are my ways your ways,"
                    declares the LORD.
                              Isaiah 55:8

F lashing lights. Orange cones. Construction workers. Mounds of dirt. Flag-clad signs: *Caution. Road closed. Detour ahead.*

Today on my drive to the YMCA, the flashing lights alerted me that I would have to travel a different route, several miles out of my way. Unexpected detours sometimes disrupt my plans and schedule. They can take me into unknown, frightening territory.

What obstruction on the road, blockade, or detour has taken you by surprise and caused you to slow down, or screech to a halt, or detour miles out of your way?

After seven years of intensive fertility treatments, Tim and Marsha faced a financial roadblock. Their savings account was depleted. Their quest for a biological child would end unless they found a way to get more money. After weighing the options of refinancing their home, selling a car, taking out a loan, or working second jobs, and after seeking truth in the Bible about debt, they decided to take a six-month break. During their time of waiting, Tim's company expanded its employee benefits program to include an adoption reimbursement plan, which they pursued and ended up getting a child the following year.

The day before Paul and Lynn were to receive their baby through a local Christian adoption agency, they received the devastating news that the birth mother had changed her mind. They grieved the loss of their child and continued to wait. Amazingly, within six months they received another call, and this time took their baby home.

Many godly people have encountered unexpected detours in their lives that God has used for spiritual good. Because of cancer, professional baseball pitcher Dave Dravecki lost his left arm and his career. God used that detour to influence countless lives through a ministry he and his wife started. When Joni Eareckson Tada survived a near-fatal accident and became a quadriplegic, her detour resulted in a worldwide ministry for people with disabilities: Joni and Friends. After my dear friends Gene and Carol Kent faced an unthinkable detour when their only son was sentenced to life in prison, Carol followed God's call to write a book, *When I Lay My Isaac Down*, to inspire people in overwhelming situations to have unshakable faith.

God has a plan and a spiritual purpose for every unexpected detour we may encounter, though we may not fully comprehend it at the time. I think of various "detours" of biblical characters.

- Jacob was called to go to Egypt.
- An angel appeared to young, unmarried Mary, to announce her divine pregnancy.
- Joseph was told his wife would have a child and he wasn't the biological father.
- Peter was called away from his fishing boats to follow the Messiah.

What do all these stories include? God's great "fear not." You may need to change your plans, but don't be derailed and don't fear the ride.

Are you frustrated or fearful as you confront an unexpected detour? Face what you fear with faith. Whatever obstruction or detour slows you down or redirects your journey is not a surprise to God. As you look to him to guide your next move, look beyond the obstacle and inconvenience to the opportunity to journey close to him.

Lord, where am I going? I thought my destination was clear, but now I'm facing an unexpected detour. My plans have screeched to a halt. Why this? Why now? I don't understand. Where are you? I feel as if you've abandoned me on the road. I don't know if I can journey on. Please comfort and embolden me with your presence. Please reveal your plans and direction. Help me see this obstruction as an opportunity. Amen.

STEPS TOWARD GROWTH

1. What unexpected detours have you faced along your roadway to have a child?
2. Read Mary's story in Luke 1:26–56. How did she respond to her unexpected detour? Invite God to give you eyes to see your unexpected detour through his eyes.
3. What opportunities and blessings do you see through your obstacle?
4. If you are at a crossroad and it is time for you to redirect your plans, imagine God speaking your name and telling you not to be afraid. Then listen for his direction.

MY PERSONAL JOURNEY

_____

_____

_____

_____

_____

My Personal Journey

_____

_____

_____

_____

_____

_____

_____

_____

_____

_____

_____

_____

_____

_____

_____

_____

_____

_____

_____

_____

_____

_____

_____

_____

_____

NEW VISION

Let us fix our eyes on Jesus, the author and perfecter of our faith.

Hebrews 12:2

GOD IS NOWHERE. At first glance you may read God is "no where." But look closer and you might see, "God is now here"! Your journey may bring you to a place where you need to take a fresh look at your situation.

Though I don't remember her name, I'll never forget the pain and sadness in the eyes of a woman who longed for a child who sought me out at a break during a conference. Blinded from disappointment and discouragement, her hope had faded. I could sense her deep anguish as she tearfully shared her most recent failed attempt to conceive a child. She was mourning the ability to have her own child. It was a dark moment for both of us. I prayed with her and asked God to heal her broken heart, to give her the desires of her heart, or to take her desire away.

"How did you know God wanted you to adopt?" she sniffled.

"I just knew!" I replied.

I recalled my childhood experience as the "mom" of my "first kid"—an orphaned goat, Puddles, whom God used to prepare my heart to adopt a child. This woman felt encouraged when she heard of my husband's initial reluctance and skepticism to adopt and how information and counseling through the Christian adoption agency changed his perspective. Above all, I told her that God had given me peace and excitement about the adoption process and my future child. During our fourteen months of adoption labor (paperwork, counseling, parenting classes, failed adoption, and waiting), I viewed myself as an expectant mother and even gave myself permission to buy new clothes.

The next day we bumped into each other in the ladies room. Squaring my shoulders I spoke boldly to her. "Do you still desire to have a child?" I asked.

"Yes!" she responded immediately.

"Then picture yourself in a spiritual sense 'pregnant' and start preparing and praying for your child. You're a mom-in-process!" I exclaimed.

She began to weep, but this time, she cried tears of joy. Her eyes sparkled with enthusiasm and hope. She sensed that God was calling her to adopt a child, and she left that day determined to follow that call.

Perhaps you too have been blinded by your circumstances. When you keep your eyes on your situation, you lose sight of the One who tells you to "keep your eyes fixed" on him. Go ahead, take a moment right now. Gaze into his eyes. What do you see? Love. Peace. Healing. Hope. Restoration. Joy. Life. Truth.

Open your eyes to his plans. Is he trying to expand your vision? Does he want you to see nontraditional ways to fulfill your longing for a child? (We'll talk about this more in the next devotion.)

Seek him—and his vision for you—with your whole heart. God will give you the desires of your heart, if your heart's desire is for him and his will. Claim for yourself the prayer I prayed with this distressed woman: "Give me the desire of my heart or take my desire away."

I'm reminded of the story of blind Bartimaeus told in Mark 10:46–52. He was sitting by the roadside begging as Jesus, his disciples, and a large crowd left the city. When he heard Jesus was passing by, he shouted, "Jesus, have mercy on me!" Although many rebuked him and told him to be quiet, his desire—to see—did not diminish (though it could have); instead, it intensified, and he shouted more.

In that moment God could have taken the blind man's desire to see away, but he didn't. Instead, he helped him see the truth that Jesus was the One who could grant his desire, and he needed to seek him (delight in him) wholeheartedly.

When Jesus stopped and asked the blind man, "What do you want me to do for you?" he replied, "I want to see!" Immediately Jesus granted his desire, and he followed Jesus along the road.

Do you sense your desire for a child getting stronger or fading? Is today the day to shout louder and seek the one who can grant your desire or to shout louder and seek the one who can remove or change your desire? **Regardless of what you sense God's plan is for your quest for a child, when you delight in him, he will open your eyes to his truth and vision.**

Lord, I'm blinded by my circumstance. I need your perspective. Heal me or heal my vision. Give me the desire of my heart or take my desire away. Forgive me for looking away from you in my times of doubt and discouragement. Open my eyes to your plan and truth. Help me to fix my eyes on you, the author and perfecter of my faith. Amen.

STEPS TOWARD GROWTH

1. How have your circumstances blinded your vision to have a child?
2. What options have you considered to have a child?
3. What new options do you sense God may be opening your eyes to consider?
4. Picture yourself spiritually pregnant with a child. What one thing can you do or purchase for your future child this week?

MY PERSONAL JOURNEY

Father God I love you. I feel blinded
by the discouragement and our situation.
Help us to see your will clearly for our lives.
Father give me the desire of my heart or
take the desire away. Forgive me for
looking away from you when I am discouraged
or disappointed. Open my eyes to your
plan + your truth. Father give both
Jay + I a sense of direction after
our phone call Monday night.
We stand on your word - Delight yourself
in the Lord and He will give you the
desires of your heart.

THE ADOPTION OPTION?

*Mordecai had a cousin named Hadassah, whom he had
brought up because she had neither father nor mother.*

Esther 2:7

After my first miscarriage, when I started talking about adoption, Rich was
hesitant. But he agreed to look into the matter. Information, counseling,
and God's leading brought him to a place where he was ready, even eager, to
redirect his plans.

I, however, always knew that I would adopt a child. (Actually, as I wrote in
Devotion 37, "Is God Punishing Me?" trying to have a child of our own was ini-
tially Rich's vision for our family.) My mother tells me that as a girl I used to
brag about adopting, though I don't remember.

Then there was that kid goat. And my brother Doug's living with us for a
year gave me a foretaste of what it meant to have a child grow *in* my heart. A
few weeks after Doug left us, I grieved the loss of our child through miscarriage.

Within a month of the time I would have delivered our first child, God
delivered a baby into our arms—a son, Jake, through a local Christian adoption
agency. Our entire "adoption labor" lasted about fourteen months and consisted
of lots of paperwork, counseling, parenting classes, becoming state certified
through "home visits" from a caseworker, being "matched" with a birth mother,
a failed adoption, more counseling, another "match," and finally receiving Jake
from his "transition" parents when he was nine days old.

I'll never forget the day we picked Jake up from the adoption agency.
Twenty of our closest friends huddled together in the downstairs lobby with

"welcome signs" and balloons. Hand in hand, Rich and I ascended the spiral staircase with diaper bag in tow and entered the room at the top of the stairs. My heart was racing as I entered the room where a professional-looking couple stood, holding a ten-pound, alert baby boy. "He's so big!" I whispered to Rich. I immediately noticed Jake's large brown eyes. Our eyes locked as I walked toward him. I was amazed that he seemed to focus and follow my every move.

Jake's transition mom (similar to a foster mom, who provided a home for Jake for several days after he left the hospital) handed him to me along with a bottle of formula. It was a surreal moment to finally hold my baby, the child I prayed for, waited for, labored for, and longed for. Moments later we descended the stairs to introduce our son and to announce his name to our cheering, applauding friends. When we arrived home later that day, our garage door sported a large sign from our neighbors, "IT'S A BOY! WELCOME HOME, JAKE!"

Since then God has called us to raise Jake as our own and to intercede for him the rest of our life. Our divine calling as Jake's parents is irrevocable.

If you are facing a turning point and if you feel convinced that God is calling you to have a family, what other options are you considering as you face the possibility that you may never have a child *under* your heart? The prayer of my wannabe-mom friend Trinka (see Devotion 2, "Wannabe Moms") was answered when she and her husband adopted a baby, Mariah. Is God calling you to consider nontraditional ways to increase the size of your family? Perhaps adoption, foster care, embryo adoption, or artificial insemination? Do you sense a child growing *in* your heart, if not *under* your heart, right now?

If you sense that God is leading you in a nontraditional direction, don't resist him. Follow him. Have faith. And in time, you too may discover a baby in need of a mother, a father, a nurturer, a discipler, a lifelong intercessor.

Lord, do you want us to pursue nontraditional ways to increase the size of our family? Open our hearts to receive your leading and respond. Help us to be willing to change. Lead us to people and resources to expand our knowledge. Redirect us with truth and fulfill your divine calling in our life. Amen.

STEPS TOWARD GROWTH

1. Reflect on the lives of Moses, Esther, and/or Jesus and those called to raise them. What nontraditional approach did God use to see that they were cared for as children?
2. What steps can you and your spouse take this month to clarify or affirm your calling to take some nontraditional route?
3. Picture yourself as a parent with a "child of your heart." What unique challenges do you think you would encounter? What fears? What joys?

MY PERSONAL JOURNEY

_____

_____

_____

_____

_____

_____

_____

_____

_____

_____

_____

_____

_____

_____

_____

Devotion 49

TAME YOUR TEMPER

*"In your anger do not sin": Do not let the sun go down while
you are still angry.*

Ephesians 4:26

The aroma of buttered popcorn and cotton candy filled the tent. White-faced clowns with ruby red noses sporting plaids, polka dots, and foot-long shoes shuffled up and down the stadium aisles. An assortment of high wires, ropes, cables, nets, and cages landscaped the center ring. Trumpets blared. Cymbals clashed. Lively music and a blackout signaled the show was about to begin. A white circle of light showcased the ring master clad in a top hat and black leather boots.

"Ladies and gentlemen, welcome to the greatest show on earth," he boomed.

Dancing dogs led the parade of exotic animals. The crowd laughed, then hushed with suspense as the light directed all eyes to the center cage in the ring. Snap. Pop. Snap. Yellow-furred tigers with black stripes hissed as they obeyed the commands of their trainer. One refused and lunged forward with a growl. He swiped his paw at his trainer. Was this really part of the act, or was the tiger finally exploding from the years of having to go along with the show?

Perhaps you can relate to the three-ring circus atmosphere. Who are you in the circus procession? The ringmaster? The spectators? The bearded lady (from too many hormones)? At times you may look at yourself and feel like a laughable, mismatched clown. Or are you standing high in the air about to take a leap onto a swinging trapeze of a new hope, trusting you will make it? Perhaps you feel disconnected from the show and sit alone in your seat as a spectator, watching others shuffle by. Sickened by the stench of exotic procedures and green-clad medical staff, you are ready to bolt from the tent when you notice the angry tiger in the ring. You sense a kindred spirit with the tiger's response to his tamer.

Though outwardly you appear tame, inwardly you sense a savage, angry beast ready to lash out. Weary from being onstage and submitting to the commands of others, you've had enough. Perhaps you growl at your spouse and hiss hurtful comments at others. Are you shaking your fist at God because you feel he has ignored your prayers and is keeping you in the cage of your circumstances? You may even refuse to cooperate with doctors or with your spouse. You may vent your anger through words, actions, busyness, depression, working too much, overeating, withholding sex, or other destructive ways. The beast of your emotions growls on despite those around you who try to calm you. Is it time to allow God to tame your temper?

God created you with a full array of emotions. Jesus understands your anger. Read about his life in Matthew, Mark, Luke, or John and note how he handled appropriate anger. Remember, he promised—and sent—his Holy Spirit to live inside of us, to help us to live a Christlike life.

Being angry is not a sin, though when you allow it to control you and hurt others it can be. Behind your beast of anger may be another cause lurking. Is disappointment, hurt, unmet expectations, betrayal, envy, pride, or jealousy really the cause of your rage? Are you mad at others, yourself, or God? Go ahead. Tell God. Let it out. Cry out to the One who understands your pain. Allow him to help you tame your temper. Allow him to heal the hurts in your life.

Lord, I'm so angry. I don't understand why I'm still in the circus ring trying to have a child when so many other adults abuse, abort, and abandon children. I'm angry at all the time and money I have to invest, the doctor's visits, inconvenience, questions, waiting, and disappointments I've endured. I'm mad at _____ *for* _____.

Please tame my temper. Look behind the beast of my anger and reveal to me what is hiding there. Empower me with your Holy Spirit today to face the truth. Forgive me for how I have hurt others. As the psalmist prayed, "Direct my footsteps according to your word; let no sin rule over me" (Psalm 119:133). Amen.

STEPS TOWARD GROWTH

1. Look at your circumstance as if it were a circus. To whom do you relate? Why?
2. How have you recently demonstrated anger? What do you think was the reason behind your anger? What can you do to address that deeper issue?
3. Do you need to ask someone for forgiveness for your treatment of him or her? How will you connect with this person this week?
4. Read Galatians 5:16–26. What can you do to make room for the fruit of the Spirit to grow in your spirit?

MY PERSONAL JOURNEY

_____

_____

_____

_____

_____

_____

_____

_____

_____

_____

Devotion 50

OUTWARD BOUND

The eye cannot say to the hand, "I don't need you!" And the head cannot say to the feet, "I don't need you!"

1 Corinthians 12:21

How does your longing to have a child affect others? Like a pebble thrown into the pond, the ripple effects of your unmet desire influences others, who also long for the child you long for. Behind you and beside you are people who care: parents, grandparents, aunts, uncles, cousins, sisters, brothers, neighbors, friends, coworkers. They may not say or do the right things, but that does not minimize their concern. If they are silent, maybe it's because they are afraid to hurt you by asking a private question. The disconnectedness you feel may not be "their problem," but yours. Are you so self-absorbed that you lose sight of their interests? Consider some of the comments I've heard from well-meaning third parties:

- "I grieved terribly over my daughter's eggs and her inability to conceive my grandchild!"
- "I want to help my son and his wife, but can't relate to what they are experiencing because I have several children."
- "My sister and I were both pregnant at the same time. She lost her baby, but I had my daughter. Feelings of guilt and sadness overwhelm me at times when I look at my daughter, knowing she should have a cousin the same age to play with."

- "I've tried to be strong for my friend and encourage her through everything she's been through. I wish I could tell her how much I hurt over her disappointments."
- "Dads are supposed to be strong and provide for their children. I feel so helpless as I watch my son and daughter-in-law want children and not be able to have them."
- "I can't relate to everything my neighbor is going through, but I can relate to some of her pain. I don't want her to think that because I adopted, that is what I will tell her to do."

Picture the faces of those connected to you and your spouse. How could the child you long for affect them and the role they represent to that child? What feelings are they experiencing over your situation? How could you initiate communication with them and give them permission to share their feelings?

When I miscarried our first child, I never stopped to consider how this loss would affect my friend who was pregnant at the same time. When her daughter was born, I visited her at the hospital. She handed me her baby and began to weep. I was utterly baffled.

"What's wrong?" I asked. As I handed her a Kleenex and cuddled her daughter, I listened. I had been totally unaware of the guilt she carried and of her silent suffering over my loss. I apologized for not being more sensitive to her pain, cried with her, and validated her pain by sharing mine. Yes, I also wished that her daughter had a playmate.

I am grateful that my friend had the courage to share with me her disappointment about the child I longed for. In a strange way, the void others felt over my first miscarriage seemed to validate my child's short life.

Perhaps others are waiting for you to give them permission to grieve the loss they feel over your lost or longed-for child. Significant days like birthdays of friends' children, Mother's Day, Father's Day, back to school, and weddings with wee ring bearers and flower girls may be a time when others with tender hearts remember your child. Are you willing to meet them where they are? Be sensitive and ask God to open your eyes to those who may need to share their hurt over your disappointment.

Lord, open my eyes to others who are hurting over the child I long for. Forgive me for not being as sensitive as I could about the ripple effect of my disappointment. Thank you for those whom you have placed in my life to support me. It's my turn to support them. Give me opportunities to connect with those who need my touch. Bring to mind today those I have wounded with my words or silence. Humble me to ask for forgiveness. Help me validate the loss they feel and give them permission to express their disappointment. Thank you for being my reconciler. Amen.

STEPS TOWARD GROWTH

1. Name friends and family members who are affected by the child you lost or long for.
2. What role or life experience is "void" because of your longed-for child?
3. Can you think of person(s) you have hurt with silence, words, or actions? How could you initiate communication with them to ask for forgiveness?
4. How could you give them permission to share their feelings and grieve over the child you long for?

MY PERSONAL JOURNEY

_____

_____

_____

_____

MY PERSONAL JOURNEY

ACCEPTING

Accepting: *to take or receive something offered;*
to reconcile oneself to; to believe.

Listen to advice and accept instruction,
and in the end you will be wise.
Many are the plans in a man's heart,
but it is the LORD's purpose that prevails.

Proverbs 19:20–21

We are therefore Christ's ambassadors, as though God were
making his appeal through us. We implore you on Christ's
behalf: Be reconciled to God.

2 Corinthians 5:20

Stop doubting and believe.

John 20:27b

" 'If you can'?" said Jesus. "Everything is possible for him
who believes."
Immediately the boy's father exclaimed, "I do believe; help me
overcome my unbelief!"

Mark 9:23–24

Devotion 51

ACCEPTING STRENGTH
FROM THE WORD

*Your word is a lamp to my feet
and a light for my path.*

Psalm 119:105

The aroma of fresh expresso filled the air as I entered my "writing office."
Tucked in a cozy corner of Starbucks with my venti latte, muffin, and laptop, I prepared to write a chapter. I opened up my Bible, as I do every day, and started to read. In a few short minutes a cheery voice interrupted me. "Hi, Kathe!"

Startled, I looked up and saw Mary Anne and Tim, an attractive couple from our church. Although I'd heard about them for years through our mutual friend Carol, I had met them only in recent years.

"What are you writing now?" Mary Anne asked.

"A book on infertility."

Tim and Mary Anne's eyes sparkled with interest.

"Have you heard our story?" they asked.

During the next two hours between sips of coffee, they told me their personal story of longing for a child for years. I was intrigued by their unshakeable faith through their journey. "How did you keep going?" I asked.

"At times it wasn't easy, especially when I thought I was pregnant but wasn't," said Mary Anne.

Tim nodded and confidently added, "God's Word got us through!"

After fourteen years of waiting on God's Word, Mary Anne conceived and had a son, James Samuel, and two years later, a daughter, Hannah Marie. As I hugged this glowing couple good-bye, I sensed God's presence, not because they got what they prayed for, but because their life demonstrated the power of God's Word to address the needs of those who read it, study it, pray with it—with a listening heart and persevering faith.

I challenge you to set aside ten minutes a day to be alone with God, reading Scripture, listening for his personal word to you, and praying. Accept the direction you receive—the strength God provides.

I've repeatedly gained strength from the story of Gideon, the hesitant hero whose story is told in Judges 6–8. When the angel of the Lord appeared to him and said, "The LORD is with you, mighty warrior," Gideon was hiding in a winepress. If Gideon was a mighty warrior, why was he so afraid?

Gideon responded: "But sir, if the LORD is with us, why has all this happened to us? Where are all his wonders that our fathers told us about?" If God was really with him, where was the miraculous evidence? Gideon's "challenge" goes on for a whole paragraph.

And how did God reply? "Gideon," he said, "go in the strength you have." Lead the army. Defeat Israel's enemy. "Am I not sending you?"

Perhaps God is calling you today to "go in the strength you have"—not because you are superwoman or highly competent in life skills or well-trained in survival skills—but because God is with you and his "strength is made perfect in [your] weakness" (2 Corinthians 12:9 KJV).

What is God trying to say to you? Invite him to speak through Scripture. Invite him to make his presence and his will known to you. Expect him to connect with you today. Wait on his Word and accept the strength he provides.

Lord, I invite you to speak to me today through your Word. Please speak to me. Give me strength to walk in the light of your Word. Encourage me with your truth. Help me look beyond my circumstances to you, accepting the strength I have—which is mine as it comes to me by and through your empowering Spirit. Amen.

STEPS TOWARD GROWTH

1. Reflect on Tim's comment, "God's Word got us through!" What Scriptures have been particularly helpful to you on your journey?
2. Read Psalm 40; 130:5; Isaiah 30:18. How does God speak to you personally through these Scriptures? Write one of the Scriptures down and carry it with you. Refer to it when you need encouragement.
3. If you don't have a regularly scheduled daily time alone with God, get out your daily calendar and commit to a specific devotional time.
4. Expect God to speak to you throughout your day. Be sensitive to Scripture, people, and circumstances you encounter. Record what happens.

MY PERSONAL JOURNEY

_____

_____

_____

_____

_____

_____

_____

_____

_____

_____

_____

_____

WHEN YOUR HAPPILY EVER AFTER NEVER COMES

Surely goodness and mercy shall follow me all the days of my life; and I shall dwell in the house of the Lord forever.
Psalm 23:6 KJV

Children were Cindy's life. As a youth pastor's wife, she and Jeff were spiritual parents to many. They had one son of their own, yet Cindy longed for a family portrait with two children. After suffering through miscarriages and an ectopic pregnancy, which nearly took her life, she sought answers and encouragement from her doctor.

It was the Friday of their youth retreat when she went to her doctor's appointment, alone. She expected an in-depth consultation with her to discuss the results of her fertility tests. What would the final word be on having more children? As usual the doctor was running late, and Cindy tried to remain calm while she waited . . . and waited . . . and waited. *Maybe the doctor had an emergency surgery*, she thought.

Finally, she queried the receptionist about her appointment. To her shock and dismay she learned that the doctor had left to go home. Cindy was outraged when she realized she had "forgotten" about her, even though she knew she was there. By now Cindy herself was behind schedule and worried that she would be left behind again if she didn't hurry to the church to rendezvous with those leaving on the retreat.

Minutes before she left on the youth group retreat, she got a call from the doctor. In a matter-of-fact tone she announced, "You will never have another child." Cindy was devastated. What good could come from the death of her hope? Where was God when this insensitive doctor forgot her? Did God really plan for her to find out this way, on the same day as the retreat, that she would never have another child?

Feeling alone in her journey, Cindy wondered why others who longed for children seemed to "live happily ever after." Each time she heard about a fertility-challenged couple, she identified with them until she discovered God had given them what they asked for.

One day a speaker confronted Cindy with her anger and told her, "When God says yes, he loves you, and when God says no, he loves you." Cindy just stared at him. She was expecting something more profound.

But she went home and pondered this simple truth. She accepted the speaker's challenge to pray, read, and reconnect with God. She read a psalm a day and wrote a daily letter to God. Several days into her journey she wrote, "All I want is *you*, God!"

This was a life-changing moment for Cindy. She desired God for who he was and not for what he could give her. Perhaps this was the "happily ever after" ending God knew she needed. Cindy was finally ready to accept God's story for her life. She realized that God often lets the natural process of life happen, and she gave herself permission to grieve her loss. She asked God to enlarge her life and make her loss count for something.

Cindy has inspired me to be thankful for "happily ever after" blessings that God has provided in various ways, not just through children. I've watched Cindy comfort hurting teenagers; organize garage sales, dinners, and boutiques to raise money for mission trips; create inspirational videos to encourage others; listen; make others laugh; share her personal failings; communicate verbally and nonverbally that you matter to her and to God. Observing Cindy as she served others in spite of her unfulfilled longing has helped me appreciate God's love and be thankful.

Are you waiting for the rest of your story to be written? If your "happily ever after" never comes, how will you choose to respond? God loves you no matter what. When he says "yes" or when he says "no," he loves you. Perhaps today is your turning point. Renew your hope in God. Read and reflect on his Word.

Pour out your heart to him, and maybe in time you, too, can say, "All I want is *you*, God!"

Lord, I want my parenting story to end "happily ever after." I don't under-stand why you are withholding the gift of a child from me. Others seem to get what they ask for, so why not me? If your answer is "no," help me to accept it and know that you love me, even if it doesn't feel like it. Speak to me through your psalms. Show me your love so that I can say, "All I want is you! You are the happily ever after I seek." Amen.

STEPS TOWARD GROWTH

1. How would you write your "happily ever after" ending?
2. Do you feel God has said "no" to you? How have you responded?
3. Like Cindy, how can you accept God's grace and demonstrate his love in specific ways as a "happily ever after" blessing to others?
4. Connect with God. Read a psalm a day. Read God's Word aloud as if he is speaking to you personally. Reflect. Write down your thoughts and note how God's truth applies to you.

MY PERSONAL JOURNEY

_____

_____

_____

_____

_____

MY PERSONAL JOURNEY

INFERTILITY ETIQUETTE

Show me your ways, O Lord,
teach me your paths;
guide me in your truth and teach me,
for you are God my Savior,
and my hope is in you all day long.

Psalm 25:4–5

M y friend Sandra, a gifted instructor and consultant, teaches people self-improvement techniques, including proper etiquette. I was intrigued when she told me about her class for teenage boys. I chuckled as I thought about a roomful of testosterone-raging boys sitting at a table with fine china and silver, learning to act like gentlemen. Manners and proper etiquette is a lost art in today's society, and I applaud my friend for making a difference in young people's lives and being a role model.

I've often wondered if I should offer to teach a class for Sandra entitled "Infertility Etiquette," though I'm not sure that I've fully mastered the proper actions or communication techniques for this unique group of people. I've learned plenty of "do's" and "don'ts" along the way, made plenty of mistakes, and acted inappropriately at times.

I've talked to so many who have shared their personal stories with me and the "improper" and "proper" ways they responded to people and situations. Perhaps you can add a few ideas to the list that follows. These points summarize some of the material we've discussed in previous devotions.

- Treat others the way you want to be treated.
- Count to ten before you scream.
- Be honest with yourself, your spouse, your doctor, and God.
- Get professional help or join a support group.
- Enlist people to pray for you.
- Forgive often.
- Educate others about infertility.
- Enlist a friend who will listen and let you talk.
- Teach friends and family what to say and how to say it to you.
- When on meds or going through procedures, be gentle with yourself.
- Say "no" to baby showers or gatherings without feeling guilty.
- Talk to your pastor about Mother's Day and Father's Day and ask your church to be sensitive to those who long for a child.
- Reward yourself with a gift or service after you go to the doctor.
- Celebrate small victories.
- Write thank-you notes to those who have encouraged you.
- Never go to bed angry with your spouse.
- Take a break. When the stress of trying to have a child is overwhelming, consider taking a couple of months off.
- Give yourself permission to express your feelings. Use a timer. Weep or vent with all of your heart for a set time.
- Keep a journal with you and use it often. Record your feelings, questions, ideas, successes, suggestions, Scriptures that encouraged you that day, quotes, and the like.
- Confront or let go of hurts. Never hold on to them.
- Plan! Plan for others to be insensitive. Plan your response to others.
- Write "I can do all things through Christ who strengthens me" (Philippians 4:13) on several 3 x 5 cards and place them in your wallet, car, mirror, and so on, to keep you focused on God's truth.
- Tell your spouse "I love you" and give him a hug daily.
- Spend at least ten minutes a day talking and listening to God.
- Laugh often. You may need to have a joke book, email humor, or a friend you enlist to give you a regular dose of humor.

Scripture teaches us any manner of lessons in God's etiquette. I think of 1 Corinthians 14:40: "Everything should be done in a fitting and orderly way." Note too 1 Corinthians 13:4–7:

> Love is patient, love is kind. It does not envy, it does not boast, it is not proud. It is not rude, it is not self-seeking, it is not easily angered, it keeps no record of wrongs. Love does not delight in evil but rejoices with the truth. It always protects, always trusts, always hopes, always perseveres.

Perhaps today is the day to accept God's teaching and put it into action. Review the Scriptures above and circle the words that speak to you. Invite God to teach you to apply his words in your life this week.

Dear Lord, help me to be a good student. Teach me how to accept where I am and learn how to respond in an appropriate way. You are my personal teacher. Help me put your words into action. Thank you for those who have willingly passed on what they have learned. Use me and my life to teach others. Amen.

STEPS TOWARD GROWTH

1. Review the infertility etiquette list above. Which suggestion(s) encourage you and would you be willing to try this week?
2. What other suggestion(s) would you like to add to the list?
3. Read Psalm 25, which includes the words "teach" and "instruct" five times. What teachings, through this psalm, 1 Corinthians 13, and other Scriptures are you ready to accept?

MY PERSONAL JOURNEY

CHILD-FREE LIVING

"Sing, O barren woman,
you who never bore a child;
burst into song, shout for joy,
you who never were in labor,
because more are the children of the desolate woman
than of her who has a husband,"
says the LORD.

Isaiah 54:1

I
s it possible that God has called you to live child-free? This is a question I've asked countless friends and acquaintances. A few have even sought my advice on whether their ultimate decision not to have children is normal and God-honoring. Some feel God "shut the door." Some got to a point where they felt "enough is enough"; they wondered if they were "playing God" with medical odds.

I believe "to be" or "not to be" a parent is a personal calling from God, though some may disagree with me. One group may pluck out the Scripture, "Be fruitful and multiply." Others may cite 1 Corinthians 12, about spiritual gifts and personalized plans. God calls some to be apostles, others prophets, and others teachers, and the Spirit empowers all for different roles and tasks. Is the calling to be a parent just a physical calling or a spiritual one?

As a young woman, my friend Jan never considered motherhood. But after she was married a second time to a wonderful man, the desire for a child, especially for a daughter, blossomed. When Jan raised the issue with her husband, she was surprised that he did not share her desire to have a child. She prayed that God would change his mind, but he did not.

Jan knew she needed her husband's support to move ahead to have a child. She surrendered her longing and asked God to show her his truth. God led her to Isaiah 53:1, "Sing, O barren woman . . . because more are the children of the desolate woman than of her who has a husband." Jan considered her situation. She thought of the many coworkers she had led to the Lord and the numerous industry colleagues she had spiritually influenced. (I *know* her influence, because I'm one of her former coworkers.) At peace with God's truth and calling in her life, Jan embraces child-free living with zeal, knowing that God is using her to birth and nurture many spiritual babies.

I know many others who feel called to live child-free—from pastors, ministry leaders, and executives to at-home women and those who work with children. Most have told me they have struggled with their role (especially in the church) and have been misunderstood. My Aunt Emily never desired children of her own, but she lavished love on her nieces and nephews. I used to "blame" her decision on harsh childhood circumstances and growing up in a large family, but now I wonder if perhaps God called Aunt Emily to be child-free so that more children could be blessed through her caring.

Have you considered the spiritual impact you have on others? Have you viewed your childlessness as an opportunity to spiritually parent others? Are you and your spouse at peace with the decision to live child-free? If not, what are you still wrestling with? It is important that you be unified in your decision. God's desire is for you to be "one" and not divided. Consider again any insights you discovered in Devotion 44, titled "Who's Calling?"

What does God's Word have to say about your situation? Try to find someone who is living child-free by choice. Ask questions and seek encouragement. God designed you. He gifted you. He has a purpose and a plan for you and your spouse. The children he may bless you with may not be from your womb, but a result of your spiritual nurture. Only God knows. Talk to him. Accept his calling, whatever that may be. To be or not to be child-free? Only God knows for sure.

Lord, are you calling me to live child-free? Is it my desire to have a child, or is it your desire implanted in my heart? Reveal your truth to me. Reveal your calling to my spouse so that we are unified. Give us peace based on your purpose for our lives. Help us embrace your truth and calling. Use us as you desire to make a spiritual impact in the lives of others. Amen.

STEPS TOWARD GROWTH

1. What burden or blessing does childlessness bring?
2. How could child-free living be misunderstood by others?
3. How does your spouse feel about living child-free?
4. Do you believe parenting is a spiritual calling? Why or why not?
5. In what other ways could you "be fruitful and multiply" in God's kingdom?

MY PERSONAL JOURNEY

_____

_____

_____

_____

_____

_____

_____

_____

_____

_____

ACCEPT THE BLESSING

The LORD longs to be gracious to you;
he rises to show you compassion.
For the LORD is a God of justice.
Blessed are all who wait for him!

Isaiah 30:18

"God bless you!" is a common statement we utter when people sneeze, but do we really mean and understand what we flippantly say? Consider the tremendous force and rate of speed air is expelled in a sneeze. Did you realize that a sneeze supposedly causes the human heart to stop beating for that brief nanosecond? With this paradox in mind, it seems appropriate to cry out to God and seek his blessing for the person who sneezed. Our usual response to the blessing? Acceptance by saying "Thank you!"

The truth is that God loves us so much he wants to bless us. He longs to be gracious to us and show us compassion. But sometimes, like a sneeze, we don't fully recognize God's blessing, so we don't accept it and say "Thank you!" As the cliché goes, "Look for a blessing in disguise." In a sense, that was a big part of Jesus' message in the Sermon on the Mount in Matthew 5, where he taught the Beatitudes (the Blessings) below:

"You're blessed when you're at the end of your rope. With less of you there is more of God and his rule.

"You're blessed when you feel you've lost what is most dear to you. Only then can you be embraced by the One most dear to you.

"You're blessed when you're content with just who you are—no more, no less. That's the moment you find yourselves proud owners of everything that can't be bought.

"You're blessed when you've worked up a good appetite for God. He's food and drink in the best meal you'll ever eat.

"You're blessed when you care. At the moment of being "care-full," you find yourselves cared for.

"You're blessed when you get your inside world—your mind and heart—put right. Then you can see God in the outside world.

"You're blessed when you can show people how to cooperate instead of compete or fight. That's when you discover who you really are, and your place in God's family.

"You're blessed when your commitment to God provokes persecution. The persecution drives you even deeper into God's kingdom.

"Not only that—count yourselves blessed every time people put you down or throw you out or speak lies about you to discredit me. What it means is that the truth is too close for comfort and they are uncomfortable. You can be glad when that happens—give a cheer, even! For though they don't like it, I do. All heaven applauds. And know that you are in good company."

Matthew 5:3–12 The Message

Look for God's blessings in disguise! Throughout your quest for a child you have been blessed, but maybe you didn't realize it until now. Take a moment right now and ask God to reveal a hidden blessing through your experience. Now, accept it by saying, "Thank you!"

Blessings are nothing to sneeze about, but the next time you do sneeze and someone says, "God bless you," remember your hidden blessings and respond by saying, "Thank you!"

Dear Lord, you long to be gracious to me and show me compassion. Often your blessings are in disguise and look different from what I think they should. Help me see life through your eyes. Reveal your hidden blessings in my life.

You have blessed me through my waiting for a child and in the following ways_____ in this journey. Thank you! Amen.

~᠑

STEPS TOWARD GROWTH

1. Read Matthew 5:3–12 (and also Luke 6:20–23) in a number of translations. Choose one or two of the "you are blessed" statements that you can't quite understand. Journal or discuss your puzzlement.
2. Choose one or two of the statements that you've come to understand through your journey of longing for a child. Thank God for the blessing you have received.
3. Write a few new statements of blessing that you can claim for yourself, based on personal experience and also on scriptural truths.

MY PERSONAL JOURNEY

My Personal Journey

_____

_____

_____

_____

_____

_____

_____

_____

_____

_____

_____

_____

_____

_____

_____

_____

_____

_____

_____

_____

_____

_____

_____

_____

_____

EMBRACING

Embracing: *to clasp in the arms; hug; to accept willingly; to adopt, include.*

You are my hiding place;
you will protect me from trouble
and surround me with songs of deliverance.

Psalm 32:7

As the mountains surround Jerusalem,
so the LORD surrounds his people
both now and forevermore.

Psalm 125:2

Devotion 56

EMBRACE TODAY

This is the day the LORD has made;
let us rejoice and be glad in it.

Psalm 118:24

For years my friend Cindy refused to shop for new clothes because she couldn't justify wearing them for just a few months while she waited to become pregnant. She postponed family photographs, waiting for the day when their family would be complete. Too often she missed moments in the present because she was so focused on the future.

Lisa wished she could turn back the hands of time and return to her twenties. If only she could change her past. She would work less and play more. She would slow down and help people in need. She would aggressively try to get pregnant. She wonders if her present and future would look different if she hadn't pursued other priorities. Perhaps she would not be childless.

Driving on the highway of life, are you staring in the rearview mirror at the line of wrong decisions following you? Or are you gazing so far down the road trying to anticipate potential traffic problems that you don't realize you are weaving all over the road and are about to crash?

Quick, put on the brakes! Slow down! Pull over to the side of the road! Stop!

Unbuckle your seat belt and get out of the car of your circumstances. Turn off the ignition. Take out the keys and get out. Open the door to the present. Inhale the air of this moment. What aromas do you smell? Breathe in. Now hold it and count to ten.

Slowly exhale. Let go of your cares and concerns as you do.

Look around. Look up. What do you see? Look closer. What colors, shapes, and objects are in view? God's creation is all around you. See the fingerprints of his work. Connect with your Creator. Thank him for what he made for you to see today. Listen to his creation. What sounds do you hear? Taste today. Sweet strawberries of opportunity, whipped cream moments drizzled with chocolate sauce of relationships. Savor the flavor of friendship. Touch the now. Feel your heart beating. Wrap your arms around what is. Embrace "I AM." Celebrate who you are today and how far you have come. Hug the here and now.

Live life to the full today! Get back into the car of your circumstance and journey on the road of life. It's okay to make a quick head check into the rearview mirror to see where you have been so you can learn from your past, adjust it, and then move on. It's normal to glance ahead to keep your faith moving in the right direction, but don't speed ahead and become so future-focused that you miss this moment's scenery. Embrace today. Hug the moments. Enjoy the now that I AM has created for you.

Lord, I want to live life to the full today! Forgive me for allowing the past and future to rob me of today. Allow me to slow down, to stop, and to look to you. Speak to me through what I see, hear, smell, taste, and touch today. Help me hug this moment. Show me the people and opportunities I have overlooked or taken for granted. Wrap your arms around me and encourage me to embrace today. Live through me, I AM. Amen.

STEPS TOWARD GROWTH

1. What future concerns or past regrets rob you of the present?
2. How can you celebrate today and enjoy this moment—its scenery and its opportunities?
3. Read Psalm 118, with an eye toward what it says about the *now*. Highlight verbs and statements that are in the present tense. In a sentence or paragraph, summarize what this psalm says to you.
4. Today allow God to speak to you through sight, smell, sound, touch, or taste. Embrace today!

MY PERSONAL JOURNEY

Devotion 57

EMBRACE ROMANCE

With God all things are possible.

Matthew 19:26

I had driven alone to the doctor's office where I had an appointment for an IUI. Once in the treatment room, I undressed and put on a gown. "Dim the lights, please," I said to the nearby nurse. "How 'bout some candles and soft music?" I added.

"We've never had a patient ask for that!" chuckled the nurse as she started the procedure.

A short time later I called Rich at work to tell him that everything had gone well. And when I arrived home, I was surprised by a florist delivering a dozen roses.

In this journey of longing for a child, I challenge you to find creative ways to keep the romance alive in your marriage. Are you worn down by a required routine that has replaced romance? By passionless performance instead of fun and spontaneity? I know the feeling.

When Rich and I faced a medical procedure to help facilitate conception, when we had to cope with others invading our intimate space, as unconventional and uncomfortable as it was at times, we predetermined that we would approach the encounter with a sense of adventure, positive attitudes, and humor. If Rich wasn't allowed to be with me during a procedure, just knowing he was nearby in the waiting room encouraged me.

You and your spouse may need to discuss what is right for you and how each of you can support the other. Stop and consider how your spouse may be feeling about a procedure or medical request. Something small and insignificant in your view may be a traumatic, humiliating experience to your spouse. Rich, frankly, didn't want me to be with him for any of his procedures. I had to remember that God created him and me—male and female—uniquely and differently. Sometimes my praying for him was the support he needed.

Over time we learned other innovative ways to encourage one another and spark romance during challenging times. I suggest:

- cards in the shower
- notes in the car
- messages on voice mail
- dinner dates to celebrate
- an extra long back rub
- a candlelit bubble bath
- an "I love you" text message
- a surprise getaway

Some of the best advice we received to keep love alive in our marriage was to ask one another a simple question: "When do you feel loved by me?"

God cares about you and your spouse and what you are going through. He understands how each of you is wired and knows exactly what the other needs not only to survive but also to feel loved. Have you ever asked him to show you how to love your spouse or show love creatively even in the midst of, well, "procedures"? Go ahead, ask him.

Perhaps you wonder if you and your spouse will ever have a normal, passionate, love life again. Hang in there. Think of this season as a time to build communication skills and to embrace creativity.

In time, you too may be passing along these words to another couple who find themselves where you are. Until then, look to the One who can do *all* things; with him *nothing* is impossible.

Lord, where is the romance in our relationship? I feel as if we are going through the medical motions, and our intimate moments have become public domain. I love my spouse, but I hate what we are going through. Change my perspective. Enlarge my thinking, my humor, my patience, my understanding of my spouse's needs, my ability to communicate my needs to my spouse, and my romantic creativity. You are the God of possibilities. Rekindle my romantic passion for my spouse. Ignite the spiritual passion in my soul for you. Amen.

STEPS TOWARD GROWTH

1. How has your experience affected your love life?
2. How have you and your spouse supported one another through this process?
3. Take time as a couple to complete the following exercise. Complete this sentence: "I feel loved when you_____." List all of your answers. Exchange lists. Do at least one item per day on the list this week to show love to your spouse.
4. Read Song of Songs 5. Ask God to kindle a fire of romance in your marriage.

MY PERSONAL JOURNEY

_____

_____

_____

_____

_____

_____

_____

_____

_____

_____

EMBRACE HUMOR

Sarah said, "God has brought me laughter."

Genesis 21:6

H ow would you like your eggs?" the waiter asked.

This routine question caught me off guard. I glanced at Rich and we both chuckled. I wondered how our waiter would react if I said, "Mature, healthy, and fertilized!"

Don't be surprised if you develop a zany sense of humor and laugh at terms and situations when others scratch their heads in bewilderment. Outsiders don't get it! Like me, you may become a bit egg crazy and view life's scenery with a new different perspective.

One time during my week of ovulation, I chose to lighten up. I changed my focus and looked for "egg things." When I spied the book *Green Eggs and Ham* at the dentist office, I erupted into laughter. During lunch with a friend I nearly choked on my water when the soup of the day was announced: egg drop soup. (I envisioned a fertility technician's nightmare.) When the grocery ad promoted, "Buy a dozen eggs, get a dozen free," I wondered how this type of promotion would work at a donor clinic.

Humor can bring healing in your journey. I realize that the circumstances, decisions, procedures—the waiting—you are facing is serious business. But you can *choose* how you are going to respond. You *do* control that. Ask God to help you look on the light side of your situation. Recently I discovered a great book of humor, *Laughin' Fertility*, for the baby-making challenged. I wish I had found the book early in my journey.

God created the gift of laughter. The Bible includes dozens of humorous situations: smelly shepherds who become kings and deliverers, a disobedient Jonah in the belly of a fish with only two possibilities to get out, a talking donkey, and an army of soldiers walking silently around Jericho. Ecclesiastes 3:4 reminds us that there is a time to weep and a time to laugh. Jesus himself says, "Blessed are you who weep now, for you will laugh" (Luke 6:21b). When God fulfilled his promise and gave Sarah a son when she was well past the age of child-bearing and her husband, Abraham, was a hundred years old, Sarah said, "God has brought me laughter, and everyone who hears about this will laugh with me" (Genesis 21:6).

Today you may choose not to laugh through your longing, but tomorrow you may cackle when an unsuspecting neighbor asks to borrow a cup of sugar and an egg. Ask God to help you look on the light side of your situation this week.

Lord, help me lighten up! I need a touch of your holy humor in my situation this week. Enlarge my vision to see with new eyes. Your Word says there is a time for laughter, and I need it now! Thank you for the thread of humor woven throughout the lives of biblical characters. You are the One who can do all things. Thank you for being the One who can transform my weeping into laughter. Amen.

STEPS TOWARD GROWTH

1. Reflect on the past couple of weeks. Identify one "infertility experience" in which you can—at least in hindsight—see some humor.

2. Read the story of Sarah in Genesis 21. What holy humor do you find here?

3. Reflect on other examples in your life or the Bible where you can see God's humor.

4. Lighten up! Become "egg-centric." This week look for examples of "egg things" and list them below. When you need a chuckle, read the list.

My Personal Journey

_____
_____
_____
_____
_____
_____
_____
_____
_____
_____
_____
_____
_____
_____
_____
_____
_____
_____
_____
_____
_____
_____
_____
_____
_____
_____
_____
_____

Devotion 59

BEAR HUG

Bear ye one another's burdens, and so fulfil the law of Christ.
Galations 6:2 KJV

At the end of a speaking engagement, I held up a large basket of stuffed bears in a variety of shapes and colors and invited anyone to come forward who needed encouragement. After hearing me describe practical ways to reach out and support others who have lost or longed for a child, a woman in Colorado mailed me the bears to give away. And now, to my surprise, several women hurried to grab a fuzzy friend.

One lone brown bear remained. *Give it to Stephanie*, I thought.

I scanned the conference room looking for the young missionary couple who had touched my heart. Even though I had met them only two days earlier, I felt a kindred connection; they had left suburbia to follow God's call to live in and serve rural America. Having grown up in a town of three hundred, I understood the challenges they faced and the need for Jesus to be taken to a small town. More important, I understood Stephanie's aching heart and empty arms. She immediately sought me out after I'd shared my journey through infertility. I'd listened, comforted, and prayed with this young woman. Yet I sensed I needed to do more.

To my amazement, I looked up and saw Stephanie traversing through the crowd toward *me*. Our eyes locked. As she approached, I grabbed the bear and gently placed it in her arms. I knew that a stuffed animal could never take the place of the child Stephanie longed for, but I wanted to validate the void she felt and fill her empty arms with the hope that someday she would hold a child, provided by God. Then I hugged her. We laughed, realizing the bear was between us.

This "bear hug moment" was significant for me. In a simple, tangible way it allowed me to reach out to another traveler on the journey, and doing so validated my years of longing. Because of my painful experience, I instinctively knew what to do: I embraced Stephanie's pain in my heart, which is what compassion is.

Each time I see a stuffed bear, I remember Stephanie, and I pray for her. I look forward to the day God replaces the bear and fills her arms with a child of his choosing. Until then, I will continue to wait, pray, and pass on more bears to those in need.

Are you in need of encouragement today? Do you need someone to validate your void and fill your empty arms? Right now Stephanie is praying for me and for you as I write this devotion. In a sense, she is the one placing a bear in the arms of both of us—you and me. My page was empty before I started. Now it is filled with hope for you to embrace. Consider yourself "hugged" from both of us today.

Perhaps today is the day to buy a bear for yourself to fill your arms with hope when you ache for a child and to encourage you to reach out to others who have empty arms. You understand what others may be going through. Your circumstances have changed you; you will never be the same. Allow your longing to enlarge you. Choose to be a person of compassion—to carry another's pain in your heart, even if only for a moment—through a hug, a prayer, or a stuffed bear.

Ask God to use your longing to lift another person in need. Make your void count for something. Reach out. Support someone today. Whom will you hug, for whom will you pray, or to whom will you give a stuffed bear?

Lord, encourage me and use me to encourage others. Fill my empty arms with hope and allow me to embrace others who need a touch. You are my God of compassion. Use my longing to enlarge my compassion for others—to experience others' pain in my heart. Show me today who has empty arms. Help me reach out to her with a hug, a prayer, or a bear in your name. Amen.

STEPS TOWARD GROWTH

1. The Bible tells us to encourage one another and "bear one another's burdens." How have others demonstrated this to you?
2. Compassion can be defined as "your pain in my heart." How has your experience enlarged your compassion for others who have empty arms?
3. How can you show compassion to another person this week and fill her arms with hope? List below those you know who long for a child. Take a moment and pray for them. Remember them throughout the year and especially on Mother's Day with a card, a call, a hug, or a bear.
4. My "bear hug" list:

MY PERSONAL JOURNEY

_____

_____

_____

_____

_____

_____

_____

_____

_____

_____

_____

Devotion 60
EMPTY WOMB! EMPTY TOMB!

I am the resurrection and the life. He who believes in me will live, even though he dies.

John 11:25

The women walked in silence toward the garden tomb. No words could express the emptiness they felt. Gut-wrenching grief. Disappointment. Sadness beyond tears. Deep questions: Why this? How would they survive now that hope had died? Would the void remain forever? Jesus' horrible death—he didn't deserve to die. Why hadn't his Father saved him?

As they approached the tomb, they were surprised. No soldiers. They had expected this final checkpoint to challenge them before giving them permission to enter and put final closure on their hope. But no obstacle remained and the door was unsealed. They could enter—be with their Lord, one last time. A sad ending to a hopeful start.

Cautiously, they peered inside. What? "He is not here! He is gone! Where is our Lord?" Suddenly two men appeared, their clothes illuminated like lightning.

"Why are you looking for the living among the dead?" they asked. "He is not here. He has risen!" Then they reminded the women of Jesus' words that had foretold his death and resurrection.

Yes, now they did remember. They hardly comprehended it all; even so, they left and ran to tell others what they'd seen and heard.

These women—they had known Jesus intimately. They had spent days listening to him. They believed him to be the Messiah. Yet how quickly they had forgotten his words and abandoned hope. Unable to see beyond the present circumstance, they had forgotten the good news Jesus had proclaimed. Perhaps their interpretation of what they thought he had meant clouded their vision to see the truth that day. Or perhaps the three days of waiting and wondering had opened their mind to faithlessness.

I don't know what caused their hope to fade, but it did. Yet, God intervened in the midst of their questions and illuminated their void with his truth. The empty tomb was part of his plans! The empty tomb represented hope, eternal life, endless joy, a forever relationship, no pain, no void, no resentment, perfection, faith to the fullest, Jesus alive in you and me.

Heaven and eternity is what may keep you motivated to continue stepping forward and growing. It does me. I look forward to greeting the children I never got to know fully here on earth as well as friends and relatives who knew Jesus personally. Having an eternal perspective about every situation in life, including the void you feel about the child you long for, may comfort you. Sure, you may continue to question and even suffer. Your womb may remain empty in spite of all you do. You may be forced to embrace your life here on earth and live it differently from how you had planned.

But I challenge you to stand at the doorway to the tomb. Look inside. What do you see? Nothing, right? Wrong. Sure, it's empty; Christ is risen. But the intangible, unseen evidence of his faith continues to work in your life and mine. So does God's miracle-working power through your empty womb. Even if you never produce a tangible child, what will you allow God to produce through your life to impact eternity through your experience of an empty womb?

Only in eternity will you ever fully understand God's perfect plan for your life. Until then, allow him to fill your empty womb with the truth of the empty tomb. Live life to the full each day. Embrace the truth of God's Word. Live with expectant hope that you will join him soon. Perhaps we will connect before heaven; if not, I hope to meet you in God's eternal garden. In heaven your longing will finally be filled with a holy, perfect love that will bloom eternally.

Lord, I may never fully understand your plan until eternity. But I know that I need you in my life. Only you can fill the spiritual void in my soul. I believe you, though innocent, died in my place, for my sins. But you proved stronger than death. You arose from the tomb. You are alive! I believe. Help my unbelief.

Lord, live in me and use me to reach out to others who have an empty womb, to bring them the hope that only you and the empty tomb can give. Help me embrace each day, opportunity, and person I meet with your eternal hope. I look forward to spending eternity with you. Amen.

STEPS TOWARD GROWTH

1. Read Luke 24: 1–12. What encouragement do you find in this resurrection story?
2. Reflect on your personal journey through longing to have a child and through this book. What questions remain? What insights have you gained? How has your longing enlarged you? In what ways have you been encouraged?
3. Thank God for the empty tomb. If you are uncertain about your eternal future and want to be confident that you will spend eternity with Jesus, in heaven, invite him into your life. Perhaps God is using your empty womb to fill your spiritual void. Embrace the empty tomb. Embrace Jesus. Embrace eternity, today!
4. Allow God to use you and your experience to help others. Embrace others who have an empty womb and long for a child in a personal, practical way this week.

MY PERSONAL JOURNEY

_____

_____

_____

MY PERSONAL JOURNEY

_____
_____
_____
_____
_____
_____
_____
_____
_____
_____
_____
_____
_____
_____
_____
_____
_____
_____
_____
_____
_____
_____
_____
_____

SPECIAL MEDITATIONS
FOR SPECIAL DAYS

S pecial occasions, holidays, and certain personal circumstances may be especially difficult for you to endure. When you encounter these times in your journey and find yourself in need of additional encouragement, turn to this section. Choose from the topics below and go to the page listed. You will be guided to read, reflect, record, and respond to additional Scripture and insights and perhaps directed to reread a devotion in this book that may offer a personal perspective on a poignant day.

WHEN YOU FACE MOTHER'S DAY

> *The LORD bless you,_____,*
>   *and keep you;*
> *the LORD make his face shine upon you*
>   *and be gracious to you;*
> *the LORD turn his face toward you*
>   *and give you peace.*

Numbers 6:24–26

Personalize this verse. Fill in the blank with your name.

Proclaim this verse. Read the Scripture slowly aloud several times.

Ponder this verse. Reflect on it. Which words, phrases, or images encourage you most today? Wait. Listen. Allow God to speak to your heart. Record your thoughts on the next page.

_____

_____

_____

Pray this verse. Offer it back to God as a personalized prayer for yourself. For example: "Lord, bless me and keep me; make your face shine upon me and be gracious to me. Turn your face toward me and give me peace."

Devotions to read: The Rose of Forgiveness (19), Does the Shoe Fit? (20), When Hope Turns to Dread (26), Your Shiloh (27), A Tale of Two Sisters (29), Bear Hug (59), Outward Bound (50).

WHEN YOU FACE FATHER'S DAY

Our Father in heaven,
hallowed be your name,
your kingdom come,
your will be done
    on earth as it is in heaven.
Give us today our daily bread.
Forgive us our debts,
    as we also have forgiven our debtors.
And lead us not into temptation,
    but deliver us from the evil one.

Matthew 5:9–12

Personalize this verse. Replace "our" and "us" with "my" and "me."

Proclaim this verse. Read the Scripture slowly aloud several times.

Ponder this verse. Reflect on it. Which words, phrases, or images encourage you most today? Wait. Listen. Allow God to speak to your heart. Record your thoughts below.

_____

_____

_____

Pray this verse. Offer it back to God as a personalized prayer of adoration, confession, thanksgiving, and intercession.

Devotions to read: A Second Opinion? (7), When Hope Turns to Dread (26), Attitude Change (43), Seasons of Surrender (45).

WHEN YOU FACE GRANDPARENTS DAY

There is a time for everything,
and a season for every activity under heaven;

a time to be born and a time to die,
a time to plant and a time to uproot,
a time to kill and a time to heal,
a time to tear down and a time to build,
a time to weep and a time to laugh,
a time to mourn and a time to dance,
a time to scatter stones and a time to gather them,
a time to embrace and a time to refrain,
a time to search and a time to give up,
a time to keep and a time to throw away,
a time to tear and a time to mend,
a time to be silent and a time to speak,
a time to love and a time to hate,
a time for war and a time for peace.

What does the worker gain from his toil? I have seen the bur-
den God has laid on men. He has made everything beautiful in
its time.

Ecclesiastes 3:1–11a

Personalize this verse. Picture yourself as the author of this Scripture.
Proclaim this verse. Read it slowly aloud several times.
Ponder this verse. Reflect on it. Which words, phrases, or images encourage
you most today? Wait. Listen. Allow God to speak to your heart. Record your
thoughts on the following page.

_____

_____

_____

Pray this verse. Offer it back to God as a personalized prayer.
Devotions to read: When Hope Turns to Dread (26), Outward Bound (50).

WHEN YOU FACE HOLIDAYS/FAMILY GATHERINGS

Jesus said, "Father, forgive them, for they do not know what they are doing."

Luke 23:34a

Therefore, as God's chosen people, holy and dearly loved, clothe yourselves with compassion, kindness, humility, gentleness and patience. Bear with each other and forgive whatever grievances you may have against one another. Forgive as the Lord forgave you. And over all theses virtues put on love, which binds them all together in perfect unity.

Let the peace of Christ rule in your hearts, since as members of one body you were called to peace.

Colossians 3:12–15a

Personalize these verses. Replace "your" and "you" with "my" and "me."

Proclaim these verses. Read them slowly aloud several times.

Ponder these verses. Reflect on them. Which words, phrases, or images encourage you most today? Wait. Listen. Allow God to speak to your heart. Record your thoughts below.

_____

_____

_____

Pray these verses. Offer them back to God as a personalized prayer.

Devotions to read: Journey to the Forest Fire (18), When Hope Turns to Dread (26), Your Shiloh (27), A Tale of Two Sisters (29), No Trespassing (31), Better Than Masking Tape (32), Guardian Angels (33), Outward Bound (50), Infertility Etiquette (53).

When You Face Baby Shower/Baby Dedications

Create in me a pure heart, O God,
and renew a steadfast spirit within me.
Do not cast me from your presence
or take your Holy Spirit from me.
Restore to me the joy of your salvation
and grant me a willing spirit, to sustain me.

Psalm 51:10–12

Personalize this verse.

Proclaim this verse. Read the Scripture slowly aloud several times.

Ponder this verse. Reflect on it. Which words, phrases, or images encourage you most today? Wait. Listen. Allow God to speak to your heart. Record your thoughts below.

_____

_____

_____

Pray this verse. Offer it back to God as a personalized prayer.

Devotions to read: When Hope Turns to Dread (26), A Tale of Two Sisters (29), Outward Bound (50).

WHEN YOU ARE OVULATING

Yet, O LORD, you are our Father.
We are the clay, you are the potter;
we are all the work of your hand.

Isaiah 64:8

Your love, O LORD, reaches to the heavens,
your faithfulness to the skies.
Your righteousness is like the mighty mountains,
your justice like the great deep.
O LORD, you preserve both man and beast.
How priceless is your unfailing love!
Both high and low among men
find refuge in the shadow of your wings.
They feast on the abundance of your house;
you give them drink from your river of delights.
For with you is the fountain of life;
in your light we see light.

Psalm 36:5–9

Personalize these verses. Replace "we" and "our" with "I" and "my."
Proclaim these verses. Read the Scripture slowly aloud several times.
Ponder these verses. Reflect on them. Which words, phrases, or images encourage you most today? Wait. Listen. Allow God to speak to your heart. Record your thoughts below.

_____

_____

_____

Pray these verses. Offer them back to God as a personalized prayer.
Devotions to read: The Aisle of Uncertainty (11), Mandatory Romantic Encounters (17), Maybe Today (22), Hope at the Bottom of the Cycle (24).

When You Start Your Period

We are hard pressed on every side, but not crushed; perplexed, but not in despair; persecuted, but not abandoned; struck down, but not destroyed. We always carry around in our body the death of Jesus, so that the life of Jesus may also be revealed in our body. For we who are alive are always being given over to death for Jesus' sake, so that his life may be revealed in our mortal body. So then, death is at work in us, but life is at work in you.

2 Corinthians 4:8–12

Personalize this verse. Replace "we," "our," and "us" with "I," "my," and "me."
Proclaim this verse. Read the Scripture slowly aloud several times.
Ponder this verse. Reflect on it. Which words, phrases, or images encourage you most today? Wait. Listen. Allow God to speak to your heart. Record your thoughts below.

_____

_____

_____

Pray this verse. Offer it back to God as a personalized prayer.
Devotions to read: When Hope Turns to Dread (26), A Tale of Two Sisters (29), Obstruction or Opportunity? (46), Tame Your Temper (49).

WHEN YOUR PREGNANCY TEST IS NEGATIVE

> *Lift your eyes and look to the heavens:*
> > *Who created all these?*
> *He who brings out the starry host one by one,*
> > *and calls them each by name.*
> *Because of his great power and mighty strength*
> > *not one of them is missing.*
> *Why do you say, O Jacob,*
> > *and complain, O Israel,*
> *"My way is hidden from the LORD;*
> > *my cause is disregarded by my God"?*
> *Do you not know?*
> > *Have you not heard?*
> *The LORD is the everlasting God,*
> > *the Creator of the ends of the earth.*
> *He will not grow tired or weary,*
> > *and his understanding no one can fathom.*
> *He gives strength to the weary*
> > *and increases the power of the weak.*
>
> > Isaiah 40:26–29

Personalize this verse. Talk directly to God. Replace "he" with "you" and "the weary" with "me."

Proclaim this verse. Read the Scripture slowly aloud several times.

Ponder this verse. Reflect on it. Which words, phrases, or images encourage you most today? Wait. Listen. Allow God to speak to your heart. Record your thoughts below.

_____

_____

_____

Pray this verse. Offer it back to God as a personalized prayer.

Devotions to read: When Hope Turns to Dread (26), A Tale of Two Sisters (29).

When Your Pregnancy Test Is Positive

My soul magnifies the Lord
    and my spirit rejoices in God my Savior,
for he has been mindful
    of the humble state of his servant.
From now on all generations will call me blessed,
    for the Mighty One has done great things for me—
    holy is his name.
His mercy extends to those who fear him,
    from generation to generation.
He has performed mighty deeds with his arm;
    he has scattered those who are proud in their inmost
        thoughts.
He has brought down rulers from their thrones
    but has lifted up the humble.
He has filled the hungry with good things
    but has send the rich away empty.
He has helped his servant Israel,
    remembering to be merciful
to Abraham and his descendants forever,
    even as he said to our fathers.

Luke 1:46b–55

Personalize this verse.

Proclaim this verse. Read the Scripture slowly aloud several times.

Ponder this verse. Reflect on it. Which words, phrases, or images encourage you most today? Wait. Listen. Allow God to speak to your heart. Record your thoughts below.

_____

_____

_____

Pray this verse. Offer it back to God as a personalized prayer.

Devotions to read: Hope and Joy (23), Hope at the Bottom of the Cycle (24).

WHEN YOU MISCARRY, HAVE A TUBAL PREGNANCY, OR LOSE YOUR INFANT

The LORD is my shepherd, I shall not be in want.
        He makes me lie down in green pastures,
he leads me beside quiet water,
        he restores my soul.
He guides me in paths of righteousness
        for his name's sake.
Even though I walk
        through the valley of the shadow of death,
I will fear no evil,
        for you are with me;
your rod and your staff,
        they comfort me.
You prepare a table before me
        in the presence of my enemies.
You anoint my head with oil;
        my cup overflows.
Surely goodness and love will follow me
        all the days of my life,
And I will dwell in the house of the LORD
        forever.

Psalm 23

For you created my inmost being;
        you knit me together in my mother's womb.
I praise you because I am fearfully and wonderfully made;
        Your works are wonderful,
        I know that full well.
My frame was not hidden from you
        when I was made in the secret place.
When I was woven together in the depths of the earth,
        your eyes saw my unformed body.

All the days ordained for me
were written in your book
before one of them came to be.

Psalm 139:13–16

Personalize these verses. Talk directly to God.

Proclaim these verses. Read the Scripture slowly aloud several times.

Ponder these verses. Reflect on them. Which words, phrases, or images encourage you most today? Wait. Listen. Allow God to speak to your heart. Record your thoughts below.

_____

_____

_____

Pray these verses. Offer them back to God as a personalized prayer.

Devotions to read: The Mountain of Surrender (42); Is God Punishing Me? (37).

WHEN YOU FACE A MEDICAL PROCEDURE

> *He will cover you with his feathers,*
> *and under his wings you will find refuge;*
> *his faithfulness will be your shield and rampart.*
>
> Psalm 91:4

> *For he will command his angels concerning you*
> *to guard you in all your ways.*
>
> Psalm 91:11

Personalize these verses. Replace "you" and "your" with "me" and "my."

Proclaim these verses. Read the Scripture slowly aloud several times.

Ponder these verses. Reflect on them. Which words, phrases, or images encourage you most today? Wait. Listen. Allow God to speak to your heart. Record your thoughts below.

_____

_____

_____

Pray these verses. Offer them back to God as a personalized prayer.

Devotions to read: What Do You Think God Wants You to Do? (10), The Mom with the Grandmother Face (14), Maybe Today (22), Your Shiloh (27), A Doctor You Can Trust (38), Infertility Etiquette (53), Embrace Romance (57).

WHEN YOUR ADOPTION FAILS

> *Who shall separate us from the love of Christ? Shall trouble
> or hardship or persecution or famine or nakedness or danger or
> sword? As it is written:*
>
> *"For your sake we face death all day long;*
> *we are considered as sheep to be slaughtered."*
>
> *No, in all these things we are more than conquerors through
> him who loved us. For I am convinced that neither death nor
> life, neither angels nor demons, neither the present nor the
> future, nor any powers, neither height nor depth nor anything
> else in all creation will be able to separate us from the love of
> God that is in Christ Jesus our Lord.*
>
> Romans 8:35–39

Personalize this verse. Talk directly to God. Replace "his" with "you" and "us" with "me."

Proclaim this verse. Read the Scripture slowly aloud several times.

Ponder this verse. Reflect on it. Which words, phrases, or images encourage you most today? Wait. Listen. Allow God to speak to your heart. Record your thoughts below.

_____
_____
_____

Pray this verse. Offer it back to God as a personalized prayer.

Devotions to read: Waiting to Cross Over (15), A Tale of Two Sisters (29).

WHEN YOU FEEL ALONE OR MISUNDERSTOOD

> *The LORD himself goes before you and will be with you; he
> will never leave you nor forsake you. Do not be afraid; do not
> be discouraged.*
>
> Deuteronomy 31:8

> *Though my father and mother forsake me,*
> *the LORD will receive me.*
> *Teach me your way, O LORD;*
> *lead me in a straight path*
> *because of my oppressors.*
>
> Psalm 27:10–11

Personalize these verses. Talk directly to God. Replace "you" with "me" in the first passage.

Proclaim these verses. Read the Scripture slowly aloud several times.

Ponder these verses. Reflect on them. Which words, phrases, or images encourage you most today? Wait. Listen. Allow God to speak to your heart. Record your thoughts below.

_____

_____

_____

Pray these verses. Offer them back to God as a personalized prayer.

Devotions to read: Waiting to Cross Over (15), Journey to the Forest Fire (18), Better Than Masking Tape (32), Guardian Angels (33), Tame Your Temper (49), Infertility Etiquette (53).

When You and Your Spouse Disagree

> *And when you stand praying, if you hold anything against anyone, forgive him, so that your Father in heaven may forgive you your sins.*
>
> Mark 11:25

> *Do not lie to each other, since you have take off your old self with its practices and have put on the new self, which is being renewed in knowledge in the image of its Creator. . . . Bear with each other and forgive whatever grievances you may have against one another. Forgive as the Lord forgave you. . . . And whatever you do, whether in word or deed, do it all in the name of the Lord Jesus, giving thanks to God the Father through him.*
>
> Colossians 3:9–10, 13, 17

> *Speak the truth in love.*
>
> Ephesians 4:15

Personalize these verses. Talk directly to God. Replace "you" with "I" or "me."

Proclaim these verses. Read the Scripture slowly aloud several times.

Ponder these verses. Reflect on them. Which words, phrases, or images encourage you most today? Wait. Listen. Allow God to speak to your heart. Record your thoughts below.

_____

_____

_____

Pray these verses. Offer them back to God as a personalized prayer.

Devotions to read: Who's to Blame? (6), What If My Spouse and I Disagree? (8), Whining in the Wilderness (16), Your Shiloh (27), Men Are from Hardware Stores, Women Are from Coffee Shops (30), Guardian Angels (33), Accepting Strength from the Word (51).

WHEN YOU FACE FINANCIAL PROBLEMS

> *Therefore I tell you, do not worry about your life, what you will eat or drink; or about your body, what you will wear. Is not life more important than food, and the body more important than clothes? Is not life more important than food, and the body more important than clothes? Look at the birds of the air; they do not sow or reap or store away in barns, and yet your heavenly Father feeds them. Are you not much more valuable than they? Who of you by worrying can add a single hour to his life?*
>
> Matthew 6:25–27

> *And my God will meet all your needs according to his glorious riches in Christ Jesus.*
>
> Philippians 4:19

Personalize these verses. Talk directly to God. Replace "your" with "my" and "you" with "me."

Proclaim these verses. Read the Scripture slowly aloud several times.

Ponder these verses. Reflect on them. Which words, phrases, or images encourage you most today? Wait. Listen. Allow God to speak to your heart. Record your thoughts below.

_____
_____
_____

Pray these verses. Offer them back to God as a personalized prayer.

Devotion to reads: When Hope Turns to Dread (26); What If My Spouse and I Disagree? (8).

When Your Doctor Disappoints You

*Be wise in the way you act toward outsiders; make the most
of every opportunity. Let your conversation be always full of
grace, seasoned with salt, so that you may know how to answer
everyone.*

Colossians 4:5–6

*I urge, then, first of all, that requests, prayers, intercession and
thanksgiving be made for everyone—for kings and all those
in authority [including your doctor]. . . .*

1 Timothy 2:1–2a

Personalize these verses. Talk directly to God. Replace "you" and "your" with "me" and "my."

Proclaim these verses. Read the Scripture slowly aloud several times.

Ponder these verses. Reflect on them. Which words, phrases, or images encourage you most today? Wait. Listen. Allow God to speak to your heart. Record your thoughts below.

_____

_____

_____

Pray these verses. Offer them back to God as a personalized prayer.

Devotions to read: Journey to the Forest Fire (18), Better Than Masking Tape (32), Guardian Angels (33), A Doctor You Can Trust (38), Tame Your Temper (49).

WHEN YOUR CHILD QUESTIONS YOU
ABOUT HAVING ANOTHER CHILD

"For I know the plans I have for you," declares the LORD,
*"plans to prosper you and not to harm you, plans to give you
hope and a future. Then you will call upon me and come and
pray to me, and I will listen to you. You will seek me and find
me when you seek me with all your heart."*

Jeremiah 29:11–12

*For there is a proper time and procedure for every matter,
though a man's misery weighs heavily upon him.
Since no man knows the future,
who can tell him what is to come?*

Ecclesiastes 8:6–7

Personalize these verses. Teach your child how to talk directly to God.

Proclaim these verses. Read the Scripture slowly aloud several times.

Ponder these verses. Reflect on them. Which words, phrases, or images encourage you most today? Wait. Listen. Allow God to speak to your heart. Record your thoughts below.

_____

_____

_____

Pray these verses. Offer them back to God as a personalized prayer.

Devotions to read: "Mommy, Will I Ever Have a Brother or Sister?" (9), Obstruction or Opportunity? (46).

WHEN YOU FACE A MORAL DILEMMA

My son, if you accept my words
    and store up my commands within you,
turning your ear to wisdom
    and applying your heart to understanding,
and if you call out for insight
    and cry aloud for understanding,
and if you look for it as for silver
    and search for it as for hidden treasure,
then you will understand the fear of the LORD
    and find the knowledge of God.
For the LORD *gives wisdom,*
    and from his mouth come knowledge and understanding.
He holds victory in store for the upright,
    he is a shield to those who walk is blameless,
for he guards the course of the just
    and protects the way of his faithful ones. . . .
Wisdom will save you from the ways of wicked men,
    from men whose words are perverse,
who leave the straight paths
    to walk in dark ways.

Proverbs 2:1–8, 12–13

See to it that no one takes you captive through hollow and deceptive philosophy, which depends on human tradition and the basic principles of this world rather than on Christ.

Colossians 2:8

Personalize these verses. Talk directly to God. Replace "your" with "my" and "you" with "me."

Proclaim these verses. Read the Scripture slowly aloud several times.

Ponder these verses. Reflect on them. Which words, phrases, or images encourage you most today? Wait. Listen. Allow God to speak to your heart. Record your thoughts below.

_____

_____

_____

Pray these verses. Offer them back to God as a personalized prayer.

Devotions to read: A Second Opinion? (7), Journey to the Forest Fire (18), Guardian Angels (33), Journey to the Wall (36).

When Someone You Know
Becomes Pregnant or Has a Baby

For where you have envy and selfish ambition, there you find disorder and every evil practice.

But the wisdom that comes from heaven is first of all pure; then peace-loving, considerate, submissive, full of mercy and good fruit, impartial and sincere. Peacemakers who sow in peace raise a harvest of righteousness.

James 3:16–18

Sing to the LORD, you saints of his;
praise his holy name.
For his anger lasts only a moment,
but his favor lasts a lifetime;
weeping may remain for a night,
but rejoicing comes in the morning.

Psalm 30:4–5

Personalize these verses. Talk directly to God, using "I" in place of "you."
Proclaim these verses. Read the Scripture slowly aloud several times.
Ponder these verses. Reflect on it. Which words, phrases, or images encourage you most today? Wait. Listen. Allow God to speak to your heart. Record your thoughts below.

———————————————————————————
———————————————————————————
———————————————————————————

Pray these verses. Offer the passages back to God as a personalized prayer.
Devotions to read: Does the Shoe Fit? (20), A Tale of Two Sisters (29), Guardian Angels (33), Tame Your Temper (49), Outward Bound (50).

SHARE YOUR STORY

But in your hearts set apart Christ as Lord. Always be pre-
pared to give an answer to everyone who asks you to give the
reason for the hope that you have. But do this with gentleness
and respect.

1 Peter 3:15

Sharing your story can be a growing part of your journey.

You may be thinking, "But it's too personal or painful"; or "Does anyone really want to listen?" I've asked these same questions and have been amazed by the people I encounter in daily life who long for children or know someone who does. God has connected me to strangers on airplanes, couples in the grocery store, next door neighbors, coworkers, family members, leaders, and friends. Even today while working on this section, the phone rang. After I answered a few questions for the event director about the upcoming retreat where I'll be speaking, the woman shared her lengthy journey of longing for a child. I listened and knew how to encourage her.

People who long for a child are all around you. Some you may know. Some you may not. God knows who they are and in his timing may connect you to them to listen, encourage, and share your story. Regardless of where you are in your journey, God can use your experience and insights to encourage another person and give eternal purpose to the pain you have endured.

Are you ready to reach out and touch someone? Are you willing to allow God to enlarge you and grow? When you share how God has worked in your life through longing for a child, you will encourage others.

My friend Carol Kent helped me to tell my story verbally and in written form through her Christian communication seminar (www.speakupwithconfidence.com) and her book *Speak Up with Confidence: A Step-by-Step Guide for Speakers* (Colorado Springs: NavPress, 1997). Both tools give a practical "how-to" approach to communicate your story. I've adapted her guidelines to help you begin writing your longing for a child story in the blank pages that follow. In a sense, "your story" will be the final devotion in this book. Picture me standing beside you right now cheering you on. Go ahead . . . you can do it!

Allow your longing to enlarge you and grow by reaching out to others.

Start with prayer! Ask for God's wisdom and discernment in what to share.

Identify one personal experience in your journey through longing for a child where God has worked through your life. Briefly share what happened.

- Where were you wondering, waiting, resenting, hoping, bracing, guarding, trusting, releasing, redirecting, accepting, or embracing?
- What emotions did you experience? Did you feel angry, confused, sad, guilty, lonely, depressed, or hopeless?
- What spiritual lesson did you learn from it? If you blamed yourself, your spouse, or your doctor, did God show you the importance of forgiveness?
- What Scripture verse or passage applies?
- How can your story encourage others? Revisit the journal sections where you responded to each devotion. Which one of your responses could lead another person to praise God?

Picture the end result of how God might use you in the life of another person. Here is one example of picturing the end result: "I want to help those who long for a child to understand the need to forgive others who have hurt them. I want to identify at least one person this week and practice forgiveness."

MY PERSONAL STORY

MY PERSONAL STORY

_____
_____
_____
_____
_____
_____
_____
_____
_____
_____
_____
_____
_____
_____
_____
_____
_____
_____
_____
_____
_____
_____
_____
_____
_____

SUGGESTED RESOURCES

MUSIC

Camp, Jeremy. "I Still Believe" and "Walk By Faith," from *Stay*, Word Music, 2002; www.jeremycamp.com

Chapman, Steven Curtis. "When Love Takes You In," from *All About Love*, Sparrow, 2003; "God Is God," "Carry You to Jesus," from *Declaration*, Sparrow, 2001; "With Hope," from *Speechless*, Sparrow, 1999; www.stevencurtischapman.com

Keaggy, Cheri. "My Faith Will Stay," "Keep On Shinin'," and "Lay It Down," from *My Faith Will Stay*, Sparrow, 1996; "Come What May," from *Let's Fly*, M2-O Records, 2001; www.cherikeaggy.com

King, Wes. "Thought You'd Be Here," from *Room Full of Stories*, Sparrow Song, 1997; www.wesking.com

Lewis, Crystal. "Beauty for Ashes," from *Beauty for Ashes*, Myrrh Records, 1996; www.crystallewis.com

Krippayne, Scott. "Sometimes He Calms The Storm," from *Wild Imagination*, Spring Hill Records; www.scottkrippayne.com

Paris, Twila. "A Visitor from Heaven," from *Beyond a Dream*, Sparrow, 1993; www.twilaparis.com

Point of Grace. "No More Pain," from *Rarities & Remixes*, Word Entertainment, 2000; www.pointofgrace.net

Rice, Chris. "Spare an Angel," from *Run the Earth, Watch the Sky*, Rocket Town, 2003; "My Prayer," from *Questions for Heaven*, Rocket Town, 2000; www.chrisrice.com

Schultz, Mark. "He Will Carry Me," "I Have Been There," from *Mark Schultz: Stories and Songs*, Word Entertainment, 2003; www.MarkSchultz.net

Thum, Pam. "God Is Good," from *Let There Be*, Benson, 2000; www.pamthum.com

Troccoli, Kathy, "Good-bye for Now," from *Corner of Eden*," Reunion Records, 1998; "A Baby's Prayer," from *Love and Mercy*, Reunion Records, 1997; www.kathytroccoli.com

Organizations

American Infertility Awareness Association: www.americaninfertility.org
Adoptive Families of America: www.adoptivefamilies.com
Christian Family Care Agency: www.cfcare.org
Focus on the Family: www.family.org
The Compassionate Friends: www.compassionatefriends.org
Hannah's Prayer Christian Support: www.hannah.org
Living without Children: www.childfree.net
MEND (Mommies Enduring Neonatal Death): www.mend.org
Rainbow Kids—international adoption information: www.rainbowkids.com
RESOLVE: www.resolve.org
SHARE Pregnancy and Infant Loss Support: www.nationalshareoffice.com
Shaohannah's Hope: www.shaohannahshope.org
Snowflakes: www.snowflakes.org
Stepping Stones, a ministry of Bethany Christian Services:
    www.bethany.org/step

Books

Chapman, Gary. *The Five Love Languages.* Chicago: Moody Press, 1996.
Dobson, James. *When God Doesn't Make Sense.* Wheaton: Tyndale , 1993.
Frank, Jan. *A Graceful Waiting*; www.janfrank.org.
Glahn, Sandra, and William Cutrer. *The Infertility Companion.* Grand Rapids: Zondervan, 2004.
_____. *When Empty Arms Become a Heavy Burden.* Nashville: Broadman & Holman, 1997.
Kent, Carol. *When I Lay My Isaac Down.* Colorado Springs: NavPress, 2004.
_____. *Secret Longings of the Heart.* Colorado Springs: NavPress, 1992.

Saake, Jenni. *Hannah's Hope.* Colorado Springs: NavPress, 2005; www.jennifer.saake.biz.

Safran, Lisa. *Laughin' Fertility.* Randolf, NJ: Koko, 1999.

Schalesky, Marlo. *Empty Womb, Aching Heart.* Minneapolis: Bethany, 2001.

Wunnenberg, Kathe. *Grieving the Child I Never Knew.* Grand Rapids: Zondervan, 2001; www.hopelifters.com.

Yancey, Philip. *Disappointment with God.* Grand Rapids: Zondervan, 1988.

_____. *Where Is God When It Hurts?* Grand Rapids: Zondervan, 1977.

FINAL THOUGHTS

My Easter flowers will be blooming soon," my mother said proudly as she pointed to the line of green stalks with bulging tops in her front yard. "I've waited all winter for them to grow," she chimed as she pulled an intruding weed.

I smiled as I looked down at my kneeling mother and imagined the row of yellow blossoms. My daydream was cut short when I realized I needed to pack for my return flight back to Arizona. I headed for the backyard clothesline. Giggles and squeals filled the air as I strolled past my toddler boys scampering through the grass. I still couldn't believe they were mine. A few minutes later I looked up and didn't see my four-year-old son, Josh. "Josh-ua," I called. He rounded the corner of the yard and charged towards me waving a stick like a sword. We played soldiers and engaged in "tickle attacks" until we were both breathless.

My mom emerged from the house. "My flowers!" she exclaimed.

I knew by the tone of Mom's voice that something was terribly wrong. I followed her to the front yard and gasped in horror. The tops of Mom's soon-to-bloom Easter flowers were chopped off and scattered on the ground. Mom took one look at Josh with the stick in his hand and knew what had happened. He confessed to the crime and told her how sorry he was. I didn't understand the depth of her disappointment at that moment, but later the three of us talked about the flowers that would not be this Easter, but hopefully would bloom later.

Ironically, this painful experience came at an appropriate time as I neared completion of this manuscript. God always seems to teach me through everyday life, so why should this surprise me? Today is Easter Sunday, God's appointed time for me to write this story. Unfortunately, my mom's Easter flowers did not bloom this year. I tried to fill her void by sending flowers, but I know it will not replace the blossoms that would have been.

Perhaps you can relate to her disappointment as you wait expectantly for your child to bloom in the garden of your life. Your longing may lead you through seasons where you wonder, resent, hope, brace, guard, trust, release, redirect, and accept until you embrace the reality that only God knows for sure if and when your child will ever be.

Even if God does bless you with a child within your heart or beneath it, your longing will continue in different ways. Jesus is the Easter Flower that gives us eternal hope and blooms forever. Only with him planted securely in the garden of your life will you be able to persevere and continue to grow.

Keep growing, dear friend. And I pray that in time God will fill your arms or your heart with a child. If not, I pray he will plant peace in your personal garden.

Thank you for taking the time to journey with me through the pages of my book into the garden of my life. I hope you have sensed God's presence and have grown. I pray that you will step forward with expectant hope no matter what season you are in and that the seed of eternal hope will continue to bloom in the garden of your life. I would love to hear from you. My website is: hopelifters.com, my email address is kathe@hopelifters.com, or write to me at P.O. Box 50995, Phoenix, AZ 85076–0995.

If you are interested in my speaking for your group, please contact www.speakupspeakerservices.com.

May God continue to enlarge your life and sprout hope in your garden.

Hugs from my heart to yours,

Kathe (Proverbs 3:5–6)

Grieving the Child I Never Knew

Kathe Wunnenberg

When the anticipation of your child's birth turns into the grief of miscarriage, tubal pregnancy, stillbirth, or early infant death, no words on earth can ease your loss. But there is strength and encouragement in the wisdom of others who have been there and found that God's comfort is real.

Having experienced three miscarriages and the death of an infant son, Kathe Wunnenberg knows the deep anguish of losing a child. *Grieving the Child I Never Knew* was born from her personal journey through sorrow. It is a wise and tender companion for mothers whose hearts have been broken—mothers like you whose dreams have been shattered and who wonder how to go on.

This devotional collection will help you grieve honestly and well. With seasoned insights and gentle questions, it invites you to present your hurts before God and to receive over time the healing that He alone can—and will—provide.

Each devotion includes:
- Scripture passage and prayer
- "Steps Toward Healing" questions
- Space for journaling
- Readings for holidays and special occasions

Hardcover 0-310-22777-1

Grieving the Loss of a Loved One

Kathe Wunnenberg

The bottom has dropped out of your life. Will the ache ever cease, the tears ever stop?

How can you go on in the face of a grief so profound?

Kathe Wunnenberg knows the terrible pain of losing your loved one and she understands that the sense of loss never really goes away. Yet as surely as God is faithful, there is hope for your broken heart to mend. There is life beyond the sorrow. As hard as it might be to believe right now, there is even the promise of joy in due season as you walk through your grief one day at a time.

Grieving the Loss of a Loved One is a collection of devotions especially for you, especially for now. You will find this book to be a wise, understanding, and comforting companion to help you grieve in the ways you must, and to encourage you that God has not forsaken you.

- Includes a Scripture passage and prayer for each devotion
- Offers readings for holidays, birthdays, and special occasions
- Provides space for journaling after each devotion

Hardcover 0-31022778-X

Pick up a copy today at your favorite bookstore!

GRAND RAPIDS, MICHIGAN 49530 USA
WWW.ZONDERVAN.COM

We want to hear from you. Please send your comm[...]
book to us in care of zreview@zondervan.com.

GRAND RAPIDS, MICHIGAN 49530 USA

WWW.ZONDERVAN.COM

We want to hear from you. Please send your comments about this book to us in care of zreview@zondervan.com. Thank you.

GRAND RAPIDS, MICHIGAN 49530 USA

WWW.ZONDERVAN.COM